The Green CEO

Leadership that Drives Profit *and* Sustainability

Lynn VanLeeuwen
Creator of Systainership™

Green Wave Publishing
Ocean View, HI
www.GreenWavePublishing.com

This book is available at special bulk quantity discounts to use as premiums and sales promotions, or for use in corporate training programs. For details, please contact: info@GreenWavePublishing.com

Systainership™ is a trademark noted throughout this book and is in the process of being registered by Lynn VanLeeuwen, Founding Partner of Sustainable Business Systems.

Disclaimer:
This book is presented solely for educational and entertainment purposes. The author and publisher are not offering it as legal, accounting, or other professional services advice. While best efforts have been used in preparing this book, the author and publisher make no representations or warranties of any kind with respect to the accuracy or completeness of the contents and specifically disclaim any implied warranties of merchantability or fitness of use for a particular purpose. Neither the author nor publisher shall be held liable or responsible to any person or entity with respect to any loss or incidental or consequential damages caused, or alleged to have been caused, directly or indirectly, by the information or programs contained herein. No warranty may be created or extended by sales representatives or written sales materials. Every company is different and the advice and strategies contained herein may not be suitable for your situation. The concepts and strategies shared in this book are not specific advice for your business. You should seek the services of a competent professional before beginning any business improvements or programs to find the right strategies for your business. Any likeness of the fictional story's characters or entities to actual persons, either living or dead, or to businesses, either existing or expired, is strictly coincidental.

Environmental Benefits Statement:
Please refer to www.TheGreenCEO.com/si.html for a complete statement of the sustainability considerations in printing this book.

Book Cover Text:
Graham Van Dixhorn, Write to Your Market, Inc.

Library of Congress Control Number: 2011925262
ISBN: 978-0-9827868-0-2

VanLeeuwen shows CEOs how to create an organization that not only delivers bottom line results but also respects stakeholders and the environment. The chapter on organizational focus for sustainability alone is worth the price of the book.

~ MICHAEL DALTON, FOUNDER, GUIDED INNOVATION GROUP, AUTHOR, *SIMPLIFYING INNOVATION*

Leadership and culture determine whether corporate responsibility is a profitable innovation or a cost center. The Green CEO *breaks down what it takes to lead a successful, sustainability-driven company and provides practical tools for creating a resilient and dynamic corporate culture.*

~ MIKHAIL DAVIS, MANAGER OF STRATEGIC SUSTAINABILITY, INTERFACEFLOR

In this insightful book, Lynn demonstrates that the path to sustainability is the same path we all need to take to create innovative, conscious and enduring businesses.

~ CHRIS MANN, CEO, GUAYAKI YERBA MATE

What are the bottom line concerns of companies wishing to remain profitable in this next century? Corporate culture, business identity, and transparency. Not what you thought? Then read this book.

~ JEFF MENDELSOHN, FOUNDER & CHAIR, NEW LEAF PAPER

Sustainability is not just about green business practices, but also bottom-line changes to the culture and conduct of your business. This system helps you create long-term viability and profitability, better products and services, and a great place to work.

~ PHIL NAIL, CTO, AISO.NET

To create a sustainable economy, we'll need not just better companies, but better leaders. The Green CEO *provides a road map to sustainability leadership. This informative and inspirational journey should be of interest to leaders—and emerging leaders—in organizations of all sizes and sectors.*

~ JOEL MAKOWER, EXECUTIVE EDITOR, GREENBIZ.COM, AUTHOR, *STRATEGIES FOR THE GREEN ECONOMY*

Sustainable development is now widely recognized as a core driving force for businesses that want to remain profitable and relevant. Integrating sustainability strategies into any organization is not an easy task. Leaders at all levels who want to truly make progress now need to develop competence as well as commitment. Lynn VanLeeuwen's book is exactly the kind of timely guidance leaders need.

~ DAVID COOK, EXECUTIVE AMBASSADOR, THE NATURAL STEP

This book is clear, concise and full of life. Is it on the right track? Heavens YES. It is a great book.

~ PATRICIA ABURDENE, SPEAKER AND COAUTHOR OF THE # 1 *NEW YORK TIMES* BEST-SELLER, *MEGATRENDS*

To my loving husband, Randy:
you've always believed in me and championed my efforts.

To my departed parents, Marion and Leslie:
for lighting my way, teaching me to have high aspirations,
and instilling faith in me, everlasting.

The sea of wisdom
continually washes in,
waiting for us to
have the courage to ride its waves.

~ LYNN VANLEEUWEN

CONTENTS

PREFACE

This book is for business leaders and executives rising to the challenge of growing their businesses profitably while making them—and the world in which they operate—more sustainable. Specifically, it guides you in determining how to adjust your leadership style and role to accomplish this. It's for those already aligned on a "green" course or those just embarking on their organization's journey toward sustainability.

The Green CEO provides guidance in the form of a system called Systainership™, which stands for System for Sustainability Leadership. It introduces new aspects of leading sustainability initiatives and revisits how tried-and-true leadership practices can also support such initiatives within your business. For your ease in learning, they're presented as a system you can refer to frequently to aid in your decision-making.

Need to Address Today's Challenges in a Comprehensive, Sustainable Way

This book was inspired by the imposing challenges and resulting overwhelm I have observed among business leaders in my client businesses and others I know through professional organizations. I saw them needing a way to recognize and communicate the sustainable potential for their organizations so they can confidently lead their company toward it as this initiative continues to thrive.

The Green CEO answers these questions for each executive:

- "How do I adapt my leadership to support the long-term and short-term sustainability of this business, including its profitability?"
- "While doing that, how can I augment my leadership to ensure this business supports the world in which it thrives?"

It gives a top-down leadership view of profitably growing a sustainable business in the midst of handling economic and governmental challenges as well as grassroots initiatives for a better world. Most important, it puts *you* in the driver's seat as you make well-informed, cohesive decisions for your business.

ACKNOWLEDGMENTS

I have been blessed to work with and learn from some extraordinary professionals over the past 20 plus years. Much of what you'll read in this book comes from artfully fusing those experiences. It has been a labor of love, but loved so much more due to the aid of so many who diligently inspired, contributed, reviewed, edited, and helped fortify the "fusions" into a cohesive book.

It's impossible to thank everyone who has contributed to my knowledge and experience over the years, but I do especially want to acknowledge the following people for their valuable information, insights, and inspiration:

Sarah Brooks of The Natural Step - Canada; David Cook, Executive Ambassador of The Natural Step International; Mike Dalton of Guided Innovation Group; Fred Forman; Peter Hopkins of Crane & Co.; Bob King, President of Pacific Biodiesel; Chris Mann, CEO of Guayaki Sustainable Rainforest Products, Inc.; Phil Nail, CTO of AISO.net; Kincey Potter; Bruce Potter, President of Island Resources Foundation; Richard Pritzlaff, President of Biophilia Foundation; Mike Taylor; Elvia Thompson; Bob Willard, Author of *The Sustainability Advantage*; and Dave Williams, former CEO of ShoreBank Pacific.

Barbara McNichol Editorial did a stellar job of editing this book, and it was a delight to work with the crew at Mullins Creative that provided the cover and interior designs. Wendy Jones and Lorna McLeod were guiding lights throughout the process.

I thank all of these wonderful people in the full spirit of *aloha*. I am proud of their contributions to this book as well as to a sustainable world through their conscious business practices.

INTRODUCTION

How does *The Green CEO* deliver leadership expertise to support you at the helm for making well-informed, cohesive decisions going forward? It acts like an armchair coach; guiding you in the face of your leadership challenges as you make your business sustainable. This introduction outlines how it is organized and the ways you can use it.

Sustainability Leadership in Five Parts

The first chapter in Part One presents the fictional case of a business executive who has lost the vision he once held for his company—a story that may evoke similarities to relevant parts of your business scenario. Chapter 2 follows with inspiring success stories that directly relate to the leadership aspects presented throughout this book while Chapter 3 provides an overview of the Systainership functions, designed to help you develop your leadership practices.

Parts Two to Four (Chapters 4-16) provide you with details of this leadership system for integrating sustainability into the core of your business. This integration aims to increase profitability and growth, create industry leadership and stewardship, and heighten an individual and collective sense of power and purpose. Several chapters include coaching questions, suggestions for action, and space to record your insights on developing sustainable practices as well as a place to record your own to-do list for applying the chapter's most relevant concepts.

Part Five (Chapter 17) and the Afterword encourage you to bring dream back into your business, just as the fictional character in Part I does. They suggest next steps you might take. Finally, a bibliography with valuable resource aids you on your journey to sustainability.

Fit the Puzzle Pieces Together

The Green CEO specifically helps leaders already convinced of the need for sustainability—those who want to get through leadership and organizational roadblocks while putting their company on a more sustainable course. If you think of business and world sustainability as parts of a jigsaw puzzle, this book shows how to fit together all the pieces, big and small.

You may choose to read this book in order or use the table of contents and index to direct you to specific issues you want to address right now. In either case, you'll find cross-referencing throughout will make it easy to find what you need. Taking on the exercises at the end of each leadership function chapter gets you to immediately apply what you've read. Accessing the resources listed will provide even greater value.

You'll find that this book's "system" approach allows you to readily see the sustainable leader's role in its entirety and assess where you are in the leadership process on any issue. The diagrams throughout help you track where you are within the system and show how a specific function relates to others. The side bar in Chapter 5 provides a key to easily read these diagrams.

Sit back with this book and get acquainted with proven guidelines that will put you on the path to sustainability. Enjoy becoming a true "green" executive. It's a journey worth taking!

PART ONE

What Challenges Are Stopping You and What You Can Do About Them

Restlessness and discontent
are the first necessities of progress.

~ THOMAS A. EDISON (1847- 1931)

CHAPTER

1

HOW IS YOUR BUSINESS AFFECTED BY TODAY'S CHALLENGES?

You need chaos in your soul
to give birth to a dancing star.

~ FRIEDRICH NIETZSCHE (1844-1900)

It's 5:00 a.m. The alarm's buzz pierces his grogginess. Sea Sweetleeder feels his gut wrench from anxiety when the issue that worries him most springs to mind. Nieu-Mart, his key customer, is releasing its sustainability requirements to all its suppliers today. Sea wants to keep the Nieu-Mart account, yet he's not sure how he'll reconfigure his business going forward.

The day he decided to supply his line of yo-yos to Nieu-Mart, he aimed to make the national sporting goods retail chain 50% of his business. He knew then he was taking a risk having one account exceed 20% of his company's portfolio. But snagging this account would *double his revenues* in two years! How could he pass it up?

Stomach still upset, he skips breakfast and grabs some coffee on his way out the door. He wants to get a jump on his hour-long commute. Picking up the newspaper in the driveway, he reads that oil prices are expected to rise 20% over the next month. Another twinge pokes him in the stomach. He decides to rework his cost projections for the next quarter when he gets to the office.

Traffic moves quickly, and Sea arrives earlier than he expects. But his plans are scuttled right away. Ed, his VP of production, is already waiting for him.

"Good morning, Sea. I know you weren't expecting me here this morning."

"Hi, Ed. What's so important to bring you here at this hour? I thought you worked late last night on the Shanghai project."

"I did, Sea. That's why I'm here. It's about the quality control for our first release of model XF360. The Shanghai factory substituted our paint specification for the frame with one containing traces of lead. I'm afraid we'll have to recall about ten thousand of them. I'm getting the lot numbers and Sally's working on a press release. We need to message this responsibly, Sea, so parents and retailers don't panic. But we do need to get this new model off the market."

Frustrated, Sea mutters a few choice obscenities as he asks, "How on earth did this get past production control?"

"I'm working on that. I should have a report by the end of the day."

The two talk for the next 30 minutes, mostly to absorb the crushing news. After Ed leaves, Sea slumps in his chair. "How can we make up for these recall losses?"

He pulls out the third-quarter and annual projections to calculate the likely impact of *all* the morning's news. After 15 minutes of adjusting figures, his secretary Alice pops her head in the doorway and announces Carlo, head of personnel. This isn't good; Carlo doesn't bother him unless the problem's big. Sea glances at the clock and realizes his extra planning time has just been shot.

"I got five resignations on my desk this morning," Carlo announces, feeling defeated. "The new manufacturing facility on the other side of town launched its recruiting effort a few weeks ago. It's opening in two weeks. I'm not sure if this is the end of the resignations or if I'll get more."

Again, Sea's stomach lurches. He's touched with anguish

and an awful sense of betrayal at the lack of loyalty among his employees. He reaches for the Rolaids® in his top right drawer.

All morning, Sea tries to settle into his routine of answering more phone calls than humanly possible, returning emails, and attending meetings. He gets interrupted every time he pulls out his projection reports. He munches on his usual deli sandwich for lunch while he meets with engineering department heads. He wants answers, dammit. Why are the new product design projects falling behind while expenses keep rising?

After the engineering heads leave, Sea tells Alice he'll be in conference and doesn't want to be disturbed. What he really wants is a time out. He pulls out his projection reports but can't concentrate. He leans back in his chair recalling how he got to this point.

Fourteen years ago, when Sea Sweetleeder received a small inheritance from his father, he combined it with his savings to start the company of his dreams. He knew running a business was risky, but the stock market had been a risky investment, too. He was determined to capitalize on his 18-year corporate experience in his own company. He'd do better looking out for his own interests—and he thought he'd have fun doing it, too.

Sea had always been fascinated by yo-yos. As a kid, he daydreamed about designs, tricks, and contests. With his capacity to visualize, it seemed natural to get a bachelor's degree in engineering. While moving up the corporate ladder, he got his master's in business administration from a local university. With his education, experience, and passion for yo-yos, he believed he had what it takes to build his own yo-yo manufacturing company.

In its first decade, his company AM-YO—named after his kids Andrew and Muriel—grew steadily and consistently. Its product line grew bigger and better with the popularity of yo-yo contests and sporting events. Four years ago, when the Nieu-Mart account was initiated, things got crazy gearing up production for a 50% increase within two years. During that time, labor costs kept rising so company leaders outsourced the manufacturing to China. Setting it up was easier than anticipated after they got past the red tape. But since then, the globalization gremlins have been lurking in the dark.

This past year saw costs rise while market prices remained constant, making Sea feel pinched from all directions. More competitors entered the market with sports celebrities sponsoring their marketing campaigns. That shifted the focus from product quality to celebrity endorsement. Now he had to ask: Who could he get to endorse AM-YO's new product? Would that person be good enough to save this ship from sinking?

For Sea personally, heading this business doesn't bring him joy the way he thought it would. His company's constantly barraged by both inside changes and global events. "The *world* now dictates where we're headed," he laments.

Gazing out the window, Sea wonders how he can turn AM-YO around. More important, he wonders what he can turn it toward. Without better people to rely on and a sense of teamwork, his hands are tied.

His stomach twinges as he thinks about today's resignations. One was his VP of manufacturing. "Didn't we have a good working relationship? What is she looking for? Why didn't she talk with me before making a move?" he mumbles in disbelief.

His mind jumps to how to improve productivity and then to the demands of his Nieu-Mart account. "Why do they want us to change our yo-yo production to be more sustainable now? I know businesses need to do their part to preserve the environment, but we need to get our feet under us before we can address this requirement. Don't we? How on earth can we start sustainability efforts with so much already on our plate?"

Sea has read some about the business benefits of sustainability. He's attended a few conferences and talked with employees about their ideas. He just doesn't know when or how to best integrate sustainability into his business. He'd spent so much time in his business, he couldn't find time to plan this out.

As his head is spinning from all these concerns, Sea hears a knock on the door. "Sea," Alice reminds him, "in twenty minutes, you're supposed to be at the university's business school of management." Alice hands him his speech. He knows he has to drive across town and deliver an introduction at this afternoon's executive seminar. He'd better get going.

As he gathers his belongings, Ed and Carlo appear simultaneously at the door. Sea excuses himself, but not before noticing the expressions on their faces. "I'll be back in two hours," he reassures them. He opens his upper right drawer, takes another of his Rolaids®, and puts the rest of the roll in his briefcase.

Sea feels slightly uncomfortable giving this talk to the business school. He tries to smile throughout, but certainly isn't smiling on the inside. He presents himself as positive and enthusiastic while feeling the weight of the world on his shoulders. He certainly isn't convinced by his own speech, which distresses him even more.

Upon his return to the office, Carlos and Ed slap him with two more resignations and confirmation that the China manufacturer is "doing its own thing" in spite of promises made when it passed all initial inspections on the new product. At the end of the day, exhausted, he puts a copy of Nieu-Mart's sustainability requirements in his briefcase and leaves the building asking, "*What* did I really want when I started this business?" Walking up to the front door of his home, he worries about what to say when his wife inevitably asks, "How was your day, honey?" His stomach flip-flops again. "Where the heck did I put my Rolaids®?"

You might not have Sea Sweetleeder's exact problems, but your leadership issues and challenges could be similar in many ways. This fictitious leader's thoughts about the benefits of sustainability were leading him in the right direction. Yet like Sea, you likely agree that striking a balance among profitable business objectives, environmental and social stewardship, and stakeholder relationships challenges even the strongest leaders.

Are you asking questions like these:

- How can I reconcile the demands for contributing to a more sustainable world and keeping my business running profitably?
- How can I increase loyalty among our employees and get them excited about working diligently toward our goals?
- How can I get our business initiatives to be *both* sustainable and profitable?
- How can I regain control of my business and make it more resilient to external events and changes?
- How can we minimize our overall risks?
- Where do we start and what measures will have the best result?
- How can I *not* feel overwhelmed about all of this and make good decisions with confidence?

Whether or not your business is in such dire straits, let this book, *The Green CEO*, be your guide. It shows you how to transform your leadership style into sustainability leadership. When you do that, you'll take your company to new horizons by successfully integrating suitable, sustainable business practices.

The Green CEO also explains how to capitalize on lessons from large companies and apply them to your small-to-medium-sized business. The next step is to re-invigorate your energy with the competitive business advantages that can be gained through sustainability. Chapter 2 gets you started.

CHAPTER

2

BRIDGING SUSTAINABILITY GAPS BRINGS MAJOR BENEFITS

Your problem is to bridge the gap
that exists between where you are now
and the goal you intend to reach.

EARL NIGHTINGALE (1921-1989)

SUSTAINABILITY GOES MAINSTREAM

It's not a question of when, but how. Seeking ways to create a sustainable world is building momentum, and the reasons vary—from fear of the future to being the right thing to do, from preserving the world for future generations to wanting a healthier lifestyle. Momentum coming from the bottom up includes employees, suppliers, and customers—people who want to have a positive effect within the realm of their job responsibilities and their personal lives, too.

Much research and literature support the top-down business case for sustainability. Among excellent resources are *The Sustainability Advantage* by Bob Willard, *Green to Gold* by Daniel C. Esty and Andrew S. Winston, *The Triple Bottom Line* by Andrew W. Savitz, and more. (See Bibliography at the end of this book.)

Most definitions of sustainability follow the theme put forth by the United Nations in 1987—that sustainability is the ability to "meet present needs without compromising the ability of future generations to meet their needs."[1]

Throughout this book, "sustainability" refers to the triple-based condition of 1) environmental regeneration, 2) community and cultural stewardship, and 3) responsible finance and sound economic development. This condition applies not only to the "world out there" but also to the sustainability of *your* business. To survive, it must meet today's needs without compromising its future longevity. Sustainability doesn't impose limits; it opens businesses to the world of greater possibilities.

Throughout this book, "sustainability" refers to the triple-based condition of 1) environmental regeneration, 2) community and cultural stewardship, and 3) responsible finance and sound economic development.

HOW COMPANIES BENEFIT FROM SUSTAINABILITY

Benefits you'll realize from steering your business on a sustainable course include:

- Greater productivity from motivated and fulfilled employees
- Lower employee attrition and its associated costs
- Lower costs due to eco-efficient operations and renewable energy sources
- Increased sales from a more dynamic brand identity and a more loyal market
- Reduced financial risks due to easier access to expansion capital and insurance
- Longer company lifespan by avoiding dependency on diminishing raw materials and resources
- Improved organizational image—and resulting beneficial partnerships—through responsibly publicizing how your business cares for the environment and the community

EXAMPLES OF SUCCESS THROUGH SUSTAINABILITY

The authors noted earlier in this chapter have built a strong business case for sustainability in their books. That will not be duplicated in this book. Presented here are scenarios that show how seven companies have reaped amazing benefits from their sustainability efforts. While these examples get your creative juices flowing, Parts Two, Three, and Four will tell you specifically how to lead your own organization to achieve similar results.

1. *Agilent Technologies*

   Agilent Technologies manufactures electronic and bio-analytical measurement devices. This multinational company continues to earn awards and receive acclaim as one of the best places to work. For two consecutive years, it's been listed as one of the Global 100 Most Sustainable Corporations in the World.[2]

   The company starts to reduce employee attrition the moment new hires are interviewed. It uses an online system that gives applicants essential information and lets them complete all forms before arriving for an interview. The system lets managers order all supplies and orientation materials for their new hires in minutes.[3] These new employees feel they're part of the team from the first moment.

   Such an integrated orientation systems is just the start for companies like Agilent to be able to increase their employee retention considerably. Agilent realizes savings from low employee turnover above and beyond the cost of its generous benefits. These include employee ownership (in countries which allow this), open door management, flex time and schedules, option to telecommute, distance training and degree programs, and relaxation and exercise facilities.

2. *Kaiser Permanente*

   Kaiser Permanente, serving more than eight million of its members in thc U.S., leads the health industry with its paperless management system available 24/7 in its medical clinics and hospitals. By reducing a need for paper, it has saved trees and storage costs for acres of medical records. The $4 billion system includes online patient medical records, billing, scheduling, and member information.[4] The benefits? Kaiser Permanente has reduced transport delays, freed up time for physicians, and improved patient care with better integration and fewer errors.[5] It has also improved doctor, nurse, and technician productivity and reduced duplicate testing and procedures because providers share access to previous results. In addition, Kaiser estimates six million members conducted online office visits in 2009[6] thus saving energy by not driving their vehicles. Other sustainability initiatives by Kaiser include greener buildings; using fixtures, supplies, and cleaners with fewer toxins; supporting local agriculture; and investing in greener IT hardware.[7]

Many of these worthwhile benefits are hard to quantify (with actual monetary "savings" still being determined[8]), but current indications are promising!

3. *Southwest Airlines*

Southwest Airlines CEO Gary Kelly says, "Our people are our single greatest strength and most enduring long-term competitive advantage."[9] While other airlines struggle to survive, Southwest is both a profitable competitor and consistently highlighted as one of the best places to work. Southwest's culture reflects its warrior spirit (hardworking, courageous, innovative), its servant's heart, and its "fun-luving" attitude. Employee benefits are expressed as "freedoms," such as the freedom to pursue good health, create financial security, travel, make a positive difference, and so on.[10] Southwest's employees are the most unionized of the airline companies with almost 85% belonging to a union, which makes this employee relationship even more amazing. Its people and systems are so productive, industry statistics boast 30% fewer employees per aircraft for Southwest than for other carriers.[11]

4. *General Electric (GE)*

General Electric (GE) has revitalized its brand identity—and its profits—with its dynamic "Ecomagination" descriptor. Previously,

GE had kept its green initiatives under cover until launching "Ecomagination" in 2005. Applying its green philosophy, GE focuses on using "cleaner" technologies to develop tomorrow's products for purifying water, generating and conserving energy, and more. Once GE declared its commitment to "making green," it realized a 17% increase in brand value.[12]

5. *New Leaf Paper*

New Leaf Paper has not only extended its lifespan by limiting its dependence on diminishing materials and resources, it's changing the whole paper industry.

The company's founder, Jeff Mendelsohn, started New Leaf in 1998 after a stint in the printing business using what was then touted as eco-friendly paper with 10-30% recycled content. He decided to do better and produce many 100% recycled content paper stocks. Today, the San Francisco firm leads a shift toward sustainability by making sustainable paper through sustainable milling processes.[13]

6. *Röhner*

William McDonough and Michael Braungart, authors of *Cradle to Cradle: Remaking the Way We Make Things*, worked with Röhner, a Swiss fabric mill, to develop biodegradable upholstery fabric in the mid-1990s. Röhner created Climatex® Lifecycle™, a compostable upholstery fabric, at the request of its customer DesignTex, which fabricates surface coverings.[14]

At the time, Röhner was considered one of the top environmentally conscious organizations in Europe.[15] Still, Swiss regulators classified Röhner fabric trimming waste as hazardous material that had to be "safely" exported for disposal.[16] When the company committed to create fabric with 100% biodegradable trimmings, it not only reworked the fiber content but also the fabric finishes.[17] The new fabric not only reduced the company's environmental risks but was of higher quality and more economical and "clean" to produce than previous fabrics. This development also eliminated a need for further regulation, another cost savings.[18]

7. *Avon*

Since its inception as a direct sales company in 1886, Avon has come a long way by dedicating itself to advancing women's health, beauty, and economic empowerment. It has a highly diverse global workforce of about 42,000 employees.

In the environmental arena, Avon put in place energy, waste, and CO_2 reduction strategies. But it's more widely recognized for improving its image through its community efforts. Specifically, Avon launched its Breast Cancer Crusade in 1992 in England and by 2009, it had spread across 55 countries.[19] Today, the Avon Walk for Breast Cancer is a renowned fundraising event.

As the world becomes more complex, the company's philanthropy has spread globally. In addition to breast cancer, Avon is active in the areas of domestic violence prevention and disaster relief. All of these efforts directly support its customer base in significant ways.

WHAT IS YOUR PATH?

You see from these examples that sustainability catalyzes business growth in many ways. "Going green" has become the latest business buzz phrase. Leaders are being catapulted to perform in an unfamiliar and innovative sustainable arena, striving for business success on new fronts with new strategies.

The approach presented in this book gives you tools to collaboratively lead your organization on its own sustainable path. Today, your business can leverage its resources like ***never*** before through sustainability partnerships. You can foster the engagement of employees, customers, suppliers, nongovernmental organizations (NGOs), and others who align with your philosophies on how to make the world better. More than that, you can partner on projects that benefit all, fueling greater efficiencies, productivity, and profitability. (Look for powerful examples in Chapter 5.)

A sustainable world is the destiny desired by all. Achieving sustainability across the globe depends on billions of people and millions of businesses doing their part. What is your leadership role in this endeavor? How can you lead your business to profitable growth while preserving our environment and communities?

Read on for specific ideas.

CHAPTER

3

MOVE FORWARD WITH CONFIDENCE USING SYSTAINERSHIP

Our Age of Anxiety is, in great part, the result of trying to do today's jobs with yesterday's tools.

MARSHALL MCLUHAN (1911-1980)

You already know that the sustainability of your business depends on the sustainability of the world, and the sustainability of the world depends on the sustainability of all businesses. You have read about proven sustainable business strategies from multiple industries. But you may be anxious about moving your company on this journey—considering where to start, how to best apply resources, and how you need to lead to reap the professed benefits. Perhaps your company doesn't seem "like" others that have succeeded, and you are concerned about the differences.

Models exist for business leadership and management styles, for minimizing environmental footprints, creating social strategies, and achieving "green" certifications. But knowing which ones to select and how to incorporate them into your business can feel overwhelming. This book provides you with a leadership model for incorporating these elements into your company's core business functions. It shows how to introduce them as well as how to shift minds and change the conduct of your business. It aids you in developing leadership practices to integrate all of these in a way that fully supports your profit-making activities. And it provides a great starting point.

THE MULTI-DIMENSIONAL FUNCTIONS OF SYSTAINERSHIP

The model advocated in this book, Systainership, is a system for sustainability leadership that synthesizes the wisdom of the ages, the philosophies of today's business leadership gurus, and 21st century sustainability strategies into a set of cohesive, integrated functions.

This multi-dimensional system addresses five levels of sustainability that are interrelated and build one on another:

1. Making changes within your business in a sustainable way. Each business change supports triple-based profitability and is supported by a cultural change process. The term "triple-based profitability" refers to profits based on a business model and operations that align with the three stewardship arenas of sustainability noted in Chapter 1: environmental regeneration, community and cultural stewardship, and responsible, sound economic development.
2. Operating your business sustainably. For example, working toward zero waste and/or a zero carbon footprint.
3. Providing sustainable services and products. For example, cleaning products that don't harm the environment, wind turbines that generate renewable energy, paper products made from sustainably harvested and renewable materials.
4. Developing your business to have a long-term, sustainable future. This includes all of the above within a sustainable and profitable business model, based on sound, sustainability methodologies and profitable business strategies. See the description of Interface, Inc.'s model presented in its vision statement in Chapter 5 as an example.
5. Contributing to the worldview of nested sustainable systems. For example, helping other companies apply industry best practices, generating more renewable energy than your company needs and feeding it into the community grid, or helping to develop sustainable infrastructure.

Figure 1 shows the breadth of company involvement for each level. They're interrelated and can build one upon another. Companies can

Systainership™

Levels of Business Sustainability

Level of Benefit	Level of Sustainability Engagement	Breadth of Sustainability Considerations and ROI Factors
Sustainable Change	Low-hanging Fruit Opportunities	Individual / Operational
Sustainable Operations	Functional	Group / System
Sustainable Products and Services	Strategic Competence	Life Cycle / Supply Chain
Sustainable Business	Sustainable Legacy	Organizational
Sustainable World	Universal Well-being	Nested Earth Systems

Figure 1

also work on different levels of sustainability at different times. These five levels plus the definition of sustainability from Chapter 2 provide the guideposts for the rest of this book.

Now, with so many resources at their disposal, it *may appear* to many that companies such as Nike, Hewlett-Packard, Walmart, and GE, can achieve sustainability more easily than most. The good news is that Systainership draws on the leadership successes of large corporations like these and then translates them into a doable system for leaders in *any* organization to follow, scaling it to their own resource levels. Each aspect of this system helps you contribute to local and worldwide sustainability in a way that's suitable for your business as it—

- ensures you look at your responsibilities through a sustainability lens.
- guides the integration of sustainability into core business strategies and functions.
- provides insight on how to relate your business to specific methodologies.
- sets up a foundation for systematically embedding sustainability into your business.

To accomplish this, the successful principles used by large organizations have been adapted for small to medium-sized businesses. You'll find them organized into logical relationships and presented as leadership functions. Each function is illustrated with a specific business example, with some being taken from large organizations to show how their success can be scaled down. Other examples show how small organizations have already scaled a sustainability leadership function to the size of their business.

Remember, all large organizations were once small and several have grown in sustainability in the process. You'll find the examples show how specific leadership principles work across a variety of business applications. The examples selected were not "judged" on their overall level of sustainability, but were chosen for how well they demonstrate a specific principle while providing a variety of business applications. Most demonstrate the integration of many sustainable business practices.

The leadership functions of Systainership are organized into these three directives:

- Build a sustainable culture.
- Set a sustainable course.
- Generate sustainable momentum.

Figure 2 demonstrates how these relate to each other. Notice the whole system is iterative. Each part of the system is outlined below and explained in detail throughout the book, using explicit system diagrams.

Remember, the system gives you, as the leader, flexibility in determining where to start your efforts. You may even select multiple starting points and concurrent projects in different stages.

Allow Systainership to support you in moving your company's sustainability along its path to success.

BUILDING A SUSTAINABLE CORPORATE CULTURE

A company's corporate culture represents the collective mindset of the company. It is reflected in the buy-in of employees and other stakeholders to the initiatives of its leaders. The level of support it receives directly correlates with the company's opportunity for success and leaders who view it with the care it deserves pave the way to a more sustainable future.

A company's corporate culture represents the collective mindset of the company. It is reflected in the buy-in of employees and other stakeholders to the initiatives of its leaders.

Your company's culture determines its modus operandi and ability to make changes during the best and worst of times. It's important for you as a leader to proactively establish a culture that supports the sustainability of the business. Through it, you also support the sustainability of the community and the environment.

Systainership™

How to Lead Your Company to a Sustainable Future

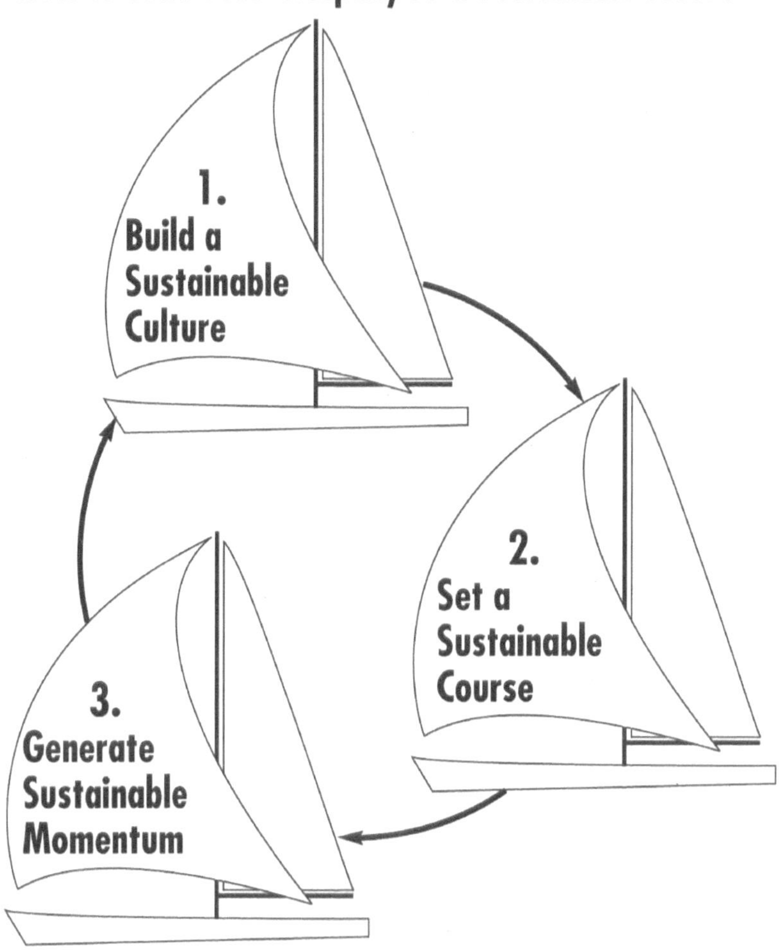

Figure 2

SETTING A SUSTAINABLE COURSE

If you have a GPS in your car, you know it requires your input on the desired destination before it can proceed. So it is with your business. Growing its size, increasing its sales, or improving its profits aren't the only destinations worth setting. In today's world, short-term gains often mean a short lifespan. Stakeholders, especially employees, crave more than a short-sighted vision statement from its leaders.

Companies facing the social, environmental, and economic challenges of this fast-paced world are spinning in circles, even those with a long-term vision of sustainability. Clearly, leaders have much to sort out . . . and so do you. Systainership helps you address the challenges and take advantage of the opportunities as you set your GPS to reach *your* long-term destination through sustainability.

GENERATING SUSTAINABLE MOMENTUM

In addition to establishing a sustainable culture and setting the direction for your company, your role also includes generating the momentum needed to create the success you've envisioned. That means it's time to drive the integration of newly acquired sustainable practices toward triple-based profitability. Systemization and communication are key to accomplishing this.

As you dive into these leadership directives, your role in establishing a sustainable culture, setting a sustainable course, and generating sustainable momentum will be explored in related functions.

WHY USE SYSTAINERSHIP?

Systainership provides a leadership approach to growing your business and a model for leading your organization. You'll be able to launch your efforts within the context of a bigger process, thus ensuring all small efforts are on the right track. You also avoid these common pitfalls:

- Having a blurred vision

- Perfecting an unsustainable business model
- Chasing a shaky market with shallow "green" proclamations
- Becoming frozen with change
- Having your business resources scattered with ineffective returns
- Missing the opportunity for new horizons for your business
- Being stymied in creating a strategy for getting from where you are to a more sustainable future for your company
- Having expensive metrics that don't meet the mark for your business
- Being paralyzed by conflicting stakeholder demands

With this complete system at hand, you'll see how to lead your company into new levels of conscious business conduct that will generate sustainable, powerful, and transformational business results. Systainership gives you the tools to simplify the complicated, get out of overwhelm, create focus, and gain confidence when making both short-term and long-term decisions. As you put in place the people, processes, and systems, you'll maximize your strengths and have more time to use your brilliance. You'll better understand what it takes to embrace change as a fluid, ongoing process. You'll also realize increased resiliency so you can weather the tides of external shifts.

. . . you'll see how to lead your company into new levels of conscious business conduct that will generate sustainable, powerful, and transformational business results.

The remaining four parts in this book guide your progress. Part Two explores the leadership functions of Systainership in building and maintaining a sustainable culture. Part Three looks at charting a sustainable course for your business. Part Four explains how to gain momentum as you integrate sustainable business practices. And Part V looks into your future as a leader.

Parts Two, Three, and Four begin with an overview chapter, followed by several detailed chapters, each representing one of the 10 core Systainership functions. At the end are tools to help you organize and assimilate the ideas presented into your business. Be sure to pause, capture, and record these core ideas before moving on. Revisit them often. Finally, Part V encourages you to envision what's possible for your business and determine what comes next for you as its leader.

By following the system presented in all parts, you'll take your organization from "believing" to "doing" in sustainable ways—ones that fit your business best.

PART TWO

Building New Solutions on a Strong Foundation

Whatever is at the center of our life
will be the source of our
security, guidance, wisdom and power.

~ STEPHEN F. COVEY (1932 -)

CHAPTER

4

HOW YOUR CORPORATE CULTURE SETS YOUR DESTINY

I respect the man who knows distinctly what he wishes. The greater part of all mischief in the world arises from the fact that men do not sufficiently understand their own aims. They have undertaken to build a tower, and spend no more labor on the foundation than would be necessary to erect a hut.

~ JOHANN WOLFGANG VON GOETHE (1749-1832)

Strong Ties in a Community Culture—a Lesson from Hershey

Hershey—Is it a town? A company? A product? Or is it a community?

The answer is yes to all. The Hershey Chocolate Company was established in 1894 to make a once-luxury item, milk chocolate, affordable to all.[20] Over generations, this leading snack food and candy manufacturer in North America has created both a strong company and community culture.

Social responsibility started with its founder, Milton Hershey. Believing that employees would be more productive if properly cared for, he bestowed paternalism by providing job stability and good schools, free healthcare, affordable housing, theaters, parks, and a zoo—all built from the proceeds of the company.[21] Today, benefits to the community provided by the Hershey company still exceed the norm.[22]

Milton also built a residential school for orphans through his personal philanthropy. This school—with more than 1600 students today—is run by the Milton Hershey School Trust, which owns controlling interest of The Hershey Company stock. The Trust plays a key role in anything affecting the value of the company[23] as does the loyalty and trust of the township, particularly stock sales and acquisitions.

In 2002, the Trust's board set up an auction to sell its Hershey stock. When poised to accept a 12.5 billion-dollar offer from the Wrigley chewing gum company, more than half the trustees had a change of heart. Protest from the townspeople, coupled with potential legal difficulties for the school trustees, squelched the deal.[24]

Continuing its founder's legacy, the company remains committed to the communities in which it operates. Milton Hershey's vision did not see beyond the town of Hershey, yet today, the company works through NGO partnerships in many locations to improve community conditions. This new approach allows the company to help each community maintain greater independence. The expanded stewardship includes sustainable cocoa farming, clean air and water management programs, reduction of greenhouse gas emissions and waste, and use of natural resources, as well as a dedication to youth.

Some advocates believe the company's partnership with ECHOES (Empowering Cocoa Households with Opportunities and Education Solutions) doesn't go far enough to protect children in the industry and want Hershey to commit to purchasing 100% fair trade chocolate. (Fair trade means purchasing from producers in underdeveloped countries under an agreement that provides livable wages and good working conditions for the workers and security to the producer. Several organizations certify fair trade companies under their own set of criteria.) However these issues get worked out, the company is extending its community care philosophy throughout the organization and supply chain.[25] And the company has become successful through the dedication of its entire community.

THE ROLE OF CULTURE IN YOUR COMPANY

Chapter 3 emphasized the importance of defining your corporate culture and understanding its role in the success of your business. If you view your culture as the modus operandi of your organization, know that the more it cultivates its culture to support its operations, the more sustainable it becomes.

Corporate culture plays many roles. It affects—

- how an organization responds to customers and competes in the market.
- what type of people get hired, promoted, or dismissed.
- how the company makes decisions regarding the challenges and opportunities it faces.
- the company's level of integrity.

In essence, the culture of your business either drives its success or leaves it floundering in the doldrums.

The Hershey story exemplifies how culture affects destiny. The company's culture was deliberately formed to support the productivity of the business and the values of its founder. What Milton didn't take into consideration was the company's long-term sustainability. Its culture became integral to the town's culture and the Milton Hershey School culture as well. As the company grew, its culture failed to evolve with it until its survival became dependant on growth beyond the town of Hershey. For many years, the company's hands were tied in determining its own fate. And although the school's trustees wanted to see the company succeed, they did not always agree on how. Today, the company's culture is evolving into one that supports a long-term, sustainable future.

Considering it's the foundation on which all operations are based, your culture needs to be as solid and supportive of its sustainable vision and long-term legacy as possible.

When you compare the resources expended to develop your culture compared to what it takes to build supporting systems and business operations, you'll realize it's a relatively small expenditure for building a foundation that will sustain the stress of a growing business. Thus, the culture needs to be developed with care and diligence. It also needs to

Correlation Between Sustainability Impact and Expended Resources
Triple-Based Profitability: Sustainable Operations
Sustainable Business Direction: The Strategies
Sustainable Culture: The Foundation
Building the Organization
Triple-Based Profitability: Sustainable Operations
Sustainable Business Direction: The Strategies
Sustainable Culture: The Foundation
Sustainability Impact: Solid Foundation on Which the Organization Rests
Expended Resources: Critical Investment on Which the Organization Balances

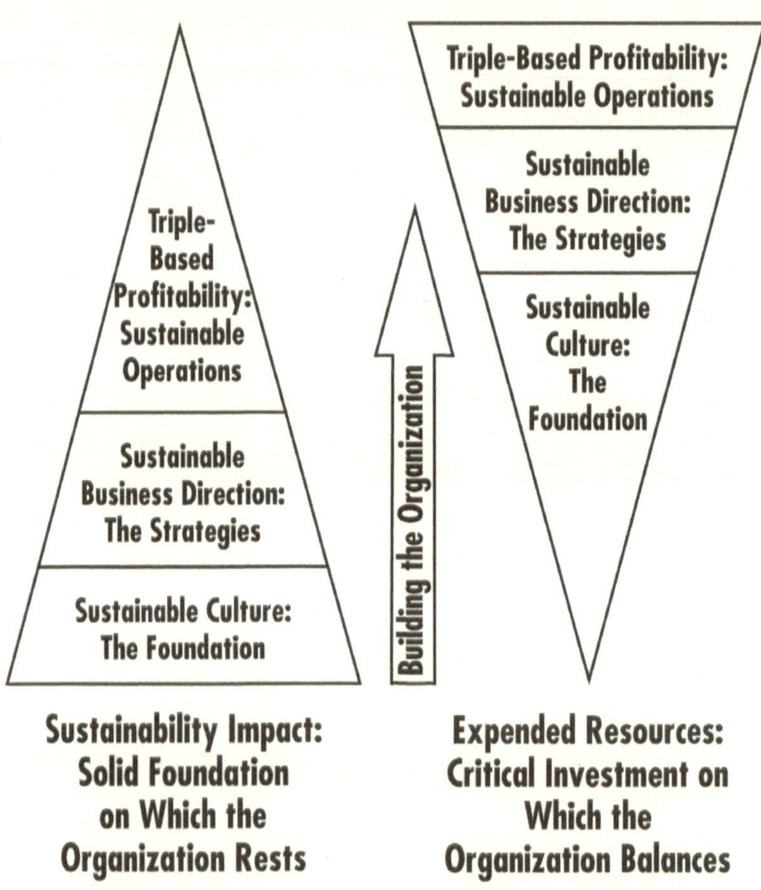

Figure 3

be congruent with your business purpose, foster its sustainability, promote its success, and support it through the tides of change. See these comparisons in Figure 3.

FACE CHANGE—EMBRACE CHANGE

How often have you been involved in creating strategic plans that were never implemented, perhaps because that gremlin voice inside your managers' heads made statements like these:

- Better not rock the boat.
- Our last major change was too tough and painful.
- I've got more important things to do.
- Just another change that won't go anywhere.

Given that the human psyche resists change, how do large organizations *embrace* change, and what lessons can be learned from those who continue to change successfully?

What if change is not something you accomplish, but rather a process within your culture? Hannah Jones, VP, Sustainable Business and Innovation at Nike, provided an example of this when she spoke for The Center for Social Innovation and Global Supply Chain Management Forum at Stanford University in 2007. Her inspiring talk described Nike's culture as "using corporate responsibility to drive innovation in the business." When I asked about the widespread acceptance of change within her organization, she said it stems from a culture that believes that failure is part of learning. After my years of coaching clients in this arena, hearing this concept was adopted by such an influential company was music to my ears.

Can you imagine striving to become an industry leader yet not being open to change? Or being in a place where mistakes are negative performance indicators rather than lessons to learn from? Or where leaders communicate only on a need-to-know basis? What mixed messages are these kinds of leaders sending?

I imagine that, during the Industrial Revolution, people in that era felt nothing had ever moved so quickly or had greater impact on economic history than during that time. In the Information Revolution,

I know people felt nothing had ever moved so quickly or had a greater impact on economic history than that era. In the midst of economic, social, and environmental crises with yet another wave of information and sustainable technologies, people feel *once again* that nothing has ever moved so quickly or had greater impact on our history than now.

The lesson? *One's perspective of both time and rate of change relates to one's own experience.*

Those who came before today's workforce accomplished great things; this generation will too. But how can the current swift rate of change be best handled? By being proactive and creative, just as those in previous generations were.

Developing a corporate culture that's proactive and creative stems from being flexible *and* having stability. Although that sounds like a paradox, it isn't. Stability can be found in what *doesn't* change—the core purpose, values, passions, and the strengths of your company and each employee. If the changes you're making align with these characteristics, you'll experience less resistance. Why? Because you're operating from what empowers you most—from the solidity of your foundation, the stability that prevails through the changing tides.

Flexibility comes from keeping your eyes open, looking around, and seeing where your business should head. You pinpoint opportunities and challenges that will affect your course; you make changes to keep those in your organization adaptable; and you use leadership strategies that make change easier and more successful. All of these become part of your company culture.

EMPOWERED PEOPLE, SOUND CULTURE

In addition to stability and flexibility, the third aspect of building a culture that embraces change is empowered people. Empowerment enables others to take on responsibility, have choice, provide input, enjoy the freedom to learn from mistakes, and receive fulfillment from what they do. Empowerment is especially important to the Y Generation, born 1977 - 2002 (or there about depending on who you listen to), with their growing numbers hitting the workforce. As a leader, you lead by modeling self-empowerment. Then, using additional leadership skills and practices discussed in the upcoming chapters, you enroll others on your company's journey.

A sound culture unifies any organization with clear, passionate vision, purpose, and values. It fosters trust, commitment, accountability, and extraordinary results. Reduced stress leads to greater productivity and lays the groundwork for a thriving legacy—a sustainable business heritage for the world. A clearly defined culture attracts better employees and often lowers employee costs. Generation Y employee applicants most often look for employment with a company that offers a sustainability program in some form.

As you contemplate making cultural changes, don't assume your existing culture is cast in stone. Invite employees to give their viewpoints. They might have great ideas that will create synergy. Spending your time listening will have a big payoff.

Your company culture isn't a set of slogans on the wall; it's a way of conducting business that's embraced throughout the organization. You reinforce this by recognizing those who fully embody it. A culture that's ingrained into the organization leads to better customer alignment. Consequently, it becomes clear *who* the company wants to do business with and *how* it wants to serve them. Empowered employees serve empowered customers. Leading by example in the embodiment of your culture further empowers those employees who are in the pipeline of sustainable leadership.

Your company culture isn't a set of slogans on the wall; it's a way of conducting business that's embraced throughout the organization.

This is how to truly *own* your company's culture.

SYSTAINERSHIP GETS RESULTS

Kotter and Heskett, authors of *Corporate Culture and Performance*, did an 11-year study of corporate cultures and found amazing results among companies that intentionally developed a supportive corporate culture. The study found these companies achieved the following results:

- An average increase in revenues of 682%
- An average workforce increase of 282%
- An average stock price growth of 901%[26]

If your small-to-medium-sized company would like to realize even a modicum of these results, then read the following three chapters. They detail the three components of building a sustainable culture within the Systainership framework. As illustrated in Figure 4, they are:

- Impart stability.
- Strengthen flexibility.
- Empower people.

You'll read about the benefits and inherent power your organization can obtain by practicing these leadership functions. You'll also explore ways to further embrace the sustainability of both your business and the world within the development of your corporate culture. And indeed, you'll notice an interplay between each of the levels of sustainability in Chapter 3 and your own business's cultural foundation.

SYSTAINERSHIP DIAGRAM KEY	
Subtitle	Systainership directive, numbered
Ship	Leadership function of Systainership, named and numbered: directive #.function #
Shaded Ship	Leadership function of Systainership being described in related text
Dashed arrow	Resources flowing from one function to another in the direction of the arrow, named
Solid arrow	Resources flowing to/from function(s) on another diagram, named, with numbers of corresponding function(s) on the other diagrams
Boxes	Resources flowing between an entity outside Systainership and a system function, named

Systainership™

1. Build a Sustainable Culture

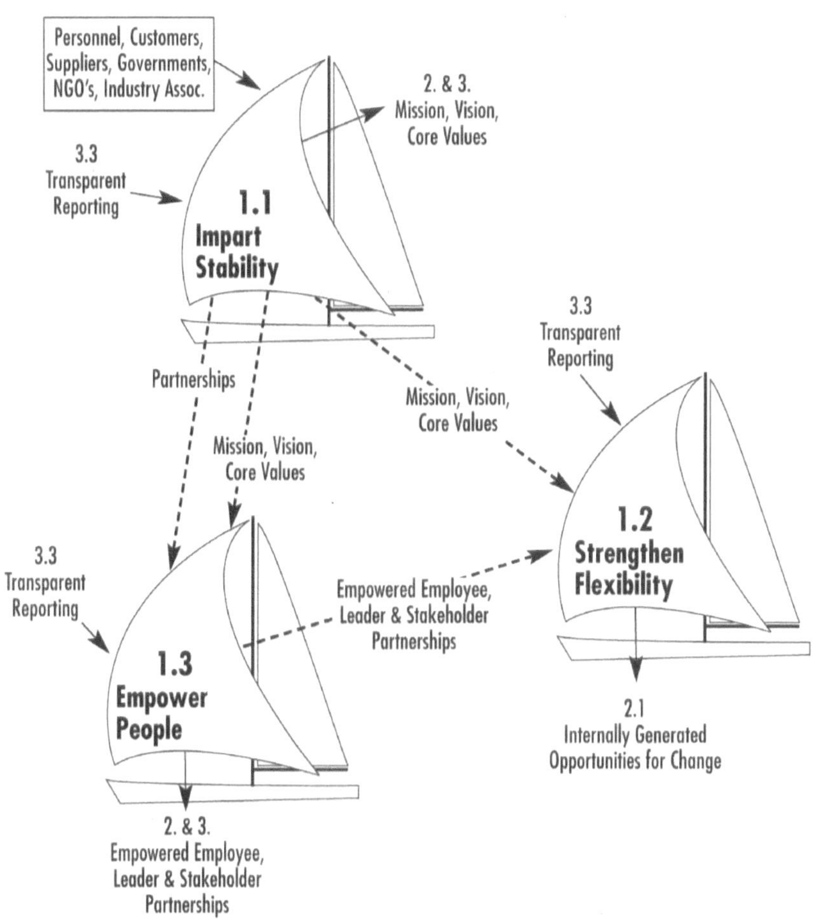

Figure 4

Your culture needs to be designed to support your business's goals. It can't be copied from another company. Remember, the more sustainable your culture, the easier it will be to achieve each of those levels of sustainability. The more sustainable your organization becomes overall, the easier it will be to maintain a sustainable culture.

Your culture needs to be designed to support your business's goals. It can't be copied from another company.

CHAPTER

5

TETHER YOUR BUSINESS TO A SOLID, SECURE LIFELINE

The hens they all cackle, the roosters all beg,
But I will not hatch, I will not hatch.
For I hear all the talk of pollution and war
As the people all shout and the airplanes roar,
So I'm staying in here, where it's safe, and it's warm,
And I will not hatch!

~ SHEL SILVERSTEIN (1930-1999)

A Solid Foundation for a Fast-Paced Dot.com—A Lesson from Zappos.com

Zappos—a play on the Spanish word "zapatos," meaning shoes—gives us a glimpse into the playfulness of this organization's culture.

Its CEO Tony Hsieh had established himself as a successful businessman at age 24 when he sold his company LinkExchange to Microsoft for $265 million.[27] But something was missing for Hsieh. He'd lost his desire to go into the office. Work had become a chore. His search for on-the-job happiness led him to other business ventures and eventually to Zappos.com. Today, he's on a quest to find a happiness theory, and he uses this company as his laboratory. It appears his experiments are proving successful!

Hsieh has molded a company in which people enjoy coming to work—so much so that the company pays less than industry average wages and doesn't match 401(k) funds. Why? Because Hsieh doesn't believe in *buying* people's happiness; he *nurtures* it through the company's culture. His philosophy presumes happy employees lead to happy customers, the ultimate goal of his business.

Although the culture at Zappos.com won't work for all companies, it fits Zappos perfectly. As evidence, the company received Fortune's "100 Best Companies to Work For" award in both 2009 and 2010.

Company leaders define Zappos as a service company that is evolving to sell anything and everything. Its mission is this:

> "One day, 30% of all retail transactions in the U.S. will be online.
>
> People will buy from the company with the best service and the best selection.
>
> Zappos.com will be that company."[28]

And its stated core values are:

> "Deliver WOW through service.
>
> Embrace and drive change.
>
> Create fun and a little weirdness.
>
> Be adventurous, creative, and open-minded.
>
> Pursue growth and learning.
>
> Build open and honest relationships with communication..."[29]

Zappos.com has undergone fast-paced changes since its 1999 beginning—from working out of Hsieh's living quarters, to its San Francisco facilities, to its Nevada facilities, and then to its warehouse in Kentucky with state-of-the-art robotic fulfillment. By its 11th year, the company grossed more than $1 billion and its staff exceeded 1,300 people. Today, besides shoes, it sells clothing, purses, and dozens of other retail items.[30]

The company's values have translated into unconventional business tactics. For example, in their first interviews, potential new employees are asked how "weird" they are to see how well they match the company's core value of creating fun and weirdness. Those who pass the interview phase go through four weeks of training that includes corporate culture and history, required book reading, and on-the-job customer service training—*no matter the position in the company.* At the end of the training period, employees are offered $2,000, in addition to their earned pay, to *leave* the company—a test of loyalty. As you can see, Zappos' leaders seek only those willing to commit to the company's journey.

Zappos employees are encouraged to read all self-help books from the company library and managers are required to spend 20% of their time with their staff outside the office. In addition, with its motto "Zappos.com—Powered by Love," employees are extensively involved in community programs, which are listed on the company's website.

In the early days of the company, Zappos used its excellence in customer service as its advertising instead of relying on expensive, conventional marketing methods. Has all this provided stability and contributed to Zappos.com's success? Yes. This service-oriented culture binds its people together, literally. Most employees attest to their satisfaction and give amazing praise to the company every year by contributing a page to its corporate culture book, which helps others learn about the company. Nurtured by this culture, employees expect to progress and be happy for years.

The success of the culture and its affect on the company is epitomized by the 2009 Amazon.com purchase of Zappos.com for stock valued at $1.2 billion.[31] Yet as Zappos.com transitioned from small to large, it maintained its culture all the way. This not only demonstrates it can be accomplished in large organizations, but it makes doing so seem more profoundly possible in small organizations. It will be interesting to watch what happens to the company culture and the success under its new ownership.

Concerning other aspects of its sustainability, Zappos controls the entire customer delivery experience, using high-level automation. It keeps the remaining jobs local rather than outsourcing them. For product fulfillment, it has energy-efficient Kiva warehouse robots programmed through sophisticated software algorithms, reducing order-to-ship time to 12 minutes. The robots can run on renewable energy, reduce employee injuries, and operate in reduced light, heat, and A/C warehouse environments. Companies such as Gap, Staples, and Crate and Barrel are following its successful lead, making Zappos.com a potential model of how to scale back outsourcing and keep future employment local.[32] Also, along the lines of sustainability, they offer several sustainable product choices including Patagonia, Smartwool, Sanuk, Bodfum, and Nvey Eco among others.

THE VALUE OF STABILITY

Sailboats use ballast in the keel to keep from getting knocked over in high winds. These days, most companies are looking for that type of stability as the winds of change blow often and fast.

Many employees feel like they just get righted when the next gust hits. And it's not only employees who experience this angst; so do all the business associates—partners, customers, vendors, stockholders, community members, and other stakeholders. For any organization, relief comes from knowing what aspects of the business can be counted on—that is, what will stay in place *no matter what* to give people a sense of security and belonging.

One source of stability employees of Zappos.com count on is having fun at their jobs. In return, they create an enjoyable experience for their customers so they'll come back for future purchases. You can see some of the fun in its YouTube TV productions such as the "random acts of kindness" parade (at www.YouTube.com do a search on "Zappos random acts of kindness"). Customer testimonials on the Zappos website also attest to how the company continually exceeds expectations and builds customer loyalty.

Think of stability as corporate comfort food. That is, when all else changes around you, corporate stability keeps you grounded; it's always supporting you. More than that, it's the ballast that keeps the ship upright when the winds of change are just chaotic.

Think of stability as corporate comfort food.

7 ELEMENTS OF STABILITY

Organizations develop stability in different ways. However, seven most commonly found elements of stability include:

1. Strong, Sustainable Mission
2. Long-term Vision
3. Organizational Core Values
4. Affinity for Partnership
5. Practice of Inclusivity
6. Principle of Sustainability
7. Protocol of Being Responsible

Let's discuss these elements one by one.

1. Strong, Sustainable Mission

A lot of confusion exists in the business world about mission and vision statements. Most companies have one or the other. Some companies that have both prioritize the *mission statement* above the *vision*; others regard the vision statement as their driving force.

For our purposes, the mission statement is defined as the *highest motivational declaration that connects to the heart and soul of the organization.* Looking at the big picture, a mission statement explains the reason *why your company exists* in a clear, concise, memorable way. Most important, it provides inspiration that's needed for day-to-day decisions and activities—the primary compass for any organization's direction, including *your* business.

Meaningful mission statements serve to encourage people's survival through hard times. Guy Kawasaki, in *The Art of the Start*, says that making meaning "is the most powerful motivator there is."[33] Lee J. Colan, author of *7 Moments that Define Excellent Leaders*, says, "Without a compelling cause, our employees are just putting in time. Their minds might be engaged, but their hearts are not."[34] That means employees are more motivated and engaged when they are aligned with a meaningful, memorable, and compelling mission.

... employees are more motivated and engaged when they're aligned with a meaningful, memorable, and compelling mission.

Some say only nonprofit organizations have a mission and, by their nature, are naturally mission-driven by a purpose that promotes a social or environmental cause. However, business leaders realize the need for a more comprehensive approach to what they do to provide greater fulfillment for those involved. Leaders of nonprofits realize that, to be sustainable, they need to adopt more businesslike economic strategies. For both types, their mission statements define their direction.

These mission statements provide powerful examples:

- Nike: "to bring inspiration and innovation to every athlete* in the world.

  *If you have a body, you are an athlete." www.Nike.com.
- One PacificCoast Bank: "... to build prosperity in our communities through beneficial banking services delivered in an economically and environmentally sustainable manner." www.opcb.com.
- Pax Scientific: Pax Scientific's mission is to translate nature's efficiencies into innovative technology applications." www.paxscientific.com.

Do you see a trend? Each one demonstrates a heartfelt connection to what the company does. These statements are inspiring, meaningful, and compelling. And so should yours be!

2. Long-term Vision

While your mission provides your company's direction, your

vision defines its destination and provides a general idea of how you'll get there. After the mission, it's the next most powerful driving force behind your company.

The statement that defines your vision can be longer than the mission statement and could include philosophical reasoning and operating principles as well as describe the ultimate state the business aims to achieve.

As a coach, when I first work with new clients, I ask them to state their long-term vision for their organizations. Their answers are often influenced by the size and flexibility of the organization—for small companies, the range of vision is usually from five to 10 years; for large organizations, it may be extended 15 to 20 years. Traditionally, they base their vision statements on forecasts of historical data and predictions of future influences and trends. These visions tend to be restricted by what company leaders see as limitations in capital, resources, markets, and so on. Experience shows that businesses with such limited views generate stagnancy. For them, it's "business as usual," growing only where they "see" a forecastable opportunity.

Today, though, historical trends aren't necessarily what leaders want to focus on. Indeed, because they create visions for the future that come from passions, desires, innovation, foresight, integrity, and stewardship, they have no historical trends from which to forecast. Instead, effective long-term vision statements paint detailed pictures of where they want to head, looking at all aspects of the business. The greater the detail, the more powerful the vision. Owners and investors used to be the only ones wanting to know a company's long-term vision. Today, *all* stakeholders demand it. They're envisioning futures that have never before

. . . because they create visions for the future that come from passions, desires, innovation, foresight, integrity, and stewardship, they have no historical trends from which to forecast.

been imagined through empowered partnerships. Then, working in partnership, they bring their visions into reality by directing their thoughts, efforts, energy, and resources toward them.

Similarly, your vision establishes the priorities and areas of focus for your business. Having a clear, long-term vision unifies energies, provides guidance for easier decision-making, and transforms the organizational energy from *pushing* against resistance to *pulling* itself into a clear opening. It also provides purpose and fulfillment for stakeholders and concentrates resources where they're needed most.

Setting sail on someone else's course won't cut it; you have to create a unique journey that aligns with your company's mission.

Setting sail on someone else's course won't cut it; you have to create a unique journey that aligns with your company's mission.

How does an organization incorporate sustainability into its vision? Sometimes sustainability is explicitly part of the mission statement; sometimes it's implied and the vision statement outlines specific sustainability principles. Or, sustainability gets implied in both statements and a list of guiding principles are developed separately.

Note these powerful examples of vision statements gleaned from the companies' websites:

- Interface, Inc.: "Interface will become the first name in commercial and institutional interiors worldwide through its commitment to people, process, product, place and profits. We will strive to create an organization wherein all people are accorded unconditional respect and dignity; one that allows each person to continuously learn and develop. We will focus on product (which includes service) through constant emphasis on process quality and engineering, which we will combine with careful attention to our customers' needs so as always to deliver superior value to our customers, thereby maximizing all stakeholders' satisfaction. We will honor the places where we do business by endeavoring to become the first name in industrial ecology, the corporation that cherishes nature and restores the environment. Interface will lead by example and validate by results, including profits, leaving the world a better place than when we began, and we will be restorative through the power of our influence in the world." www.interfaceglobal.com.

- Haworth: "Haworth will be a sustainable corporation. We engage our employees in more sustainable practices; we initiate and use processes that are neutral or improve our environment; and we utilize our resources in ways that create adaptable and sustainable workplace solutions for our customers. We do all of this globally to protect and restore our environment, create economic value, and support and strengthen our communities." www.haworth.com.
- Pax Scientific: "We envision a world in which the Pax Streamlined Principal provides benefits to every pertinent industry by developing tools that use less energy and materials while simultaneously offering greater productivity and control." www.paxscientific.com.

Notice that these statements have no specific timeline; they articulate a vision for how they see their companies presently and in the future *as a way of being* (plus some basic operating principles). These vision statements not only drive their organizations to success; they transparently inform and inspire their stakeholders—and they influence company leaders everywhere.

3. *Organizational Core Values*

Core values—beliefs and behaviors unique to an organization—aren't listed on the cafeteria wall to be ignored. Rather, they define how a company practices its business. These values get embedded into every aspect of a sustainable business.

Chip Conley, author of *Marketing That Matters*, believes core values *become* the business brand—that is, the stronger the values become "branded," the greater affinity the company will have with its customers. He states that core values should meet or *exceed* what the customer wants, bringing the customer into self-actualization. As an example of self-actualization, think back to Zappos.com's 10 core values with many of them aimed at providing their customers with fun, WOW experiences.

To compare, look at these three sets of stated organizational core values:

- The Home Depot: "… taking care of our people, giving back to our communities, doing the right thing, excellent customer service, creating shareholder value, building strong relationships, entrepreneurial spirit and respect for all people." www.homedepot.com.
- Joie de Vivre Hotels: "Fresh, Inventive, Grassroots, Casual, Experience-driven" www.jdvhotels.com.
- Pax Scientific: "The continued cultivation of the Streamlining Principal, efficient and effective business practices, a commitment to commercial success for ourselves and our business partners, streamlined communication and a recognition that every success is powered by people." www.paxscientific.com.

Notice that the core values of these companies contrast sharply with each other, leaving it up to the leaders of each one to set up the best modus operandi. Remember, the key to stability includes the full set—mission, vision, and core values—as part of any organization that wants to increase its sustainability.

For continuity, you'll notice that each of the elements of mission, vision, and core values appears above for Pax Scientific. Do you see how each builds upon and supports the other?

4. Affinity for Partnership

A partnership is a defined relationship among one or more people or entities. You may laugh at the idea of partnering with yourself, but that's a great starting point for learning how to develop meaningful partnerships. How many people really partner with themselves to accomplish their goals?

Partnership calls for defining the commitment, keeping

promises, and having integrity, trust, respect—and a loyalty and passion for your cause. Partnerships are not simply two people forming a legal entity to conduct business together; today's partnerships come with far greater advantages.

Savvy businesses form all types of partnerships—with employees, vendors, customers, industry affiliates, shareholders and other investors, communities, advocacy groups, governments, and nonprofit organizations. Traditionally, any of these groups were viewed as adversaries in these ways:

- Employees were human resources to be managed and allocated.
- Vendors were to be negotiated with to get the best price and delivery options.
- Customers were to be won over to achieve sales.
- Industry affiliates were to be handled cautiously to protect company secrets.
- Shareholders were to be appeased with regular dividends or increases in stock values.
- Communities were used to extract as much value for the company as possible.
- Advocacy groups were to be hushed and "damage controlled."
- Governments were to be lobbied to minimize impact and compliance.
- Nonprofit organizations were coffered tax deductible contributions to create a philanthropic image.

In contrast, partnerships can benefit every-one tremendously when they're interwoven and creatively designed. Today, companies often partner with many stakeholders on a single project. For example, a manufacturer could work through a nonprofit organization, an investor group, its

. . . partnerships can benefit everyone tremendously when they're interwoven and creatively designed.

employees, an advocacy program, and other industry affiliates to roll out product beta tests in an underserved community. This closely aligns with—and leverages the resources and talents of—all groups for a common purpose.

This model new partnership features such characteristics as open communication, commitment, integrity, trust, loyalty, respect and passion for the shared causes benefiting all members. These new partnerships can have various scopes. The scope could be—

- global—e.g., Clinton Global Initiative.
- regional—e.g., HP, Microsoft, and Assisted Technology Industry Assoc. partnering to break down barriers to information and technology for people with disabilities.
- local—e.g., city government, residents, and businesses partnering to build infrastructure.

Businesses also partner with vendors to provide more sustainable source materials and services for their products. Some companies partner with customers to build loyalty. An example is Patagonia, which partners with its customers through its online participatory programs for recycling clothing (Common Threads Garment Recycling), for getting product reviews, and for invoking customer action through its posted environmental essays.

An added benefit is that many partnerships can leverage minimal resources to achieve great results. In the example featuring Patagonia, two of its customer partnerships are successfully accomplished online at minimal expense.

5. Practice of Inclusivity

Inclusivity takes business relationships *beyond* partnership and recognizes that everything on this earth and beyond is related. A mindset of inclusivity brings this recognition into practice when making choices and developing strategies in your business. Other species naturally recognize their interconnectedness while humans, in their "struggle" to survive, set up protective walls and create a life of "I, me, mine." Indeed, the whole concept of win-lose sets two entities against each other.

Even organizations and individuals with worthy missions and goals find it difficult to practice inclusivity. They inadvertently set up ideological silos that create separation. For example, nonsmokers (philosophically if not physically) separate themselves from smokers. Members of environmental organizations see themselves as separate from nonmembers, standing up against all others for the rights of endangered species, as another example.

Inclusivity requires re-examining relatedness, sharing abundance, practicing compassion, inviting diversity, and working together to learn ways to thrive. Forming win-win relationships reinforces this.

You can enter the realm of inclusivity by asking questions such as these:

- Who else can win with us?
- Who else will be affected by what we do?
- Who and what will be affected by our lack of action?
- How can we permeate the barriers that prevent others from benefiting?
- How can this be *Creating a World that Works for All?* as Sharif Abdullah's book title states?

Proponents of sustainable business practices build their own silos based on judgments of level of greenness. However, *everyone* should feel invited on the journey to create a sustainable world. No one should be judged as "more advanced" nor should righteous attitudes be allowed to alienate others on similar journeys. Responsible communication of sustainable progress will tell each story.

What does inclusivity mean for *your* business? It means the potential for fewer adversaries and more people on your team. It means greater leveraging of resources. It means barriers broken and possibilities realized sooner. It means larger communities tout the work of your business to your potential market. It means greater fulfillment for all those within your organization. And it means a more stable environment in which to conduct your business.

6. Principle of Sustainability

Chapter 2 defined sustainability and Chapter 3 outlined the levels of sustainability as they might apply to your business and to the world itself. Operating sustainably means *being a social and environmental steward of the world while conducting a profitable business.* This is referred to as a green business with profitability based on social stewardship, environmental regeneration, and sound economic development.

For many companies, sustainability is such an important core value that it takes the marquee position in their mission or vision for their business; for others, it drives value without the headline status. Yet to be sustainable, it's critical to highlight "sustainability" as a core value. More than that, it's necessary to embed sustainability into every function of your organization and throughout your business model.

When population density and growth were lower than they are today, individual human needs, wants, and demands were also lower. Consequently, many businesses enjoyed a natural longevity without having a sustainable business model. Their time in history placed them at the pioneering edge of mass production and mass consumption—perhaps a mandatory educational phase our society had to pass through before we could realize the potential harm. But just like we can't have light without darkness or happiness without sorrow, we likely can't come to our current sustainability concepts without some permanent injury. Thankfully, each era has allowed us to move toward improved business models and technologies. And now, the time has come for *sustainable* business invention!

... it's necessary to embed sustainability into every function of your organization and throughout your business model.

Being sustainable and operating sustainably go hand in hand. Think of it as a lens, not a silo. Like profitability, it's not a function of the organization but a cornerstone of your business model and a consideration in every aspect of it. Adopt this holistic approach and it will strengthen the profitability, health, and well-being of your company *and* the world in which it operates. (Chapter 7 explores sustainability factors within business models in detail.)

7. *Protocol of Being Responsible*

What's the difference between having responsibilities and being responsible?

In terms of having responsibilities, some are assigned (e.g., managers designating tasks to employees); some are inherited (e.g., parenting or taking someone else's position); some are self-imposed (e.g., completing college, supporting your church, or volunteering to train new recruits).

The responsibilities of business leaders broaden as they take on the responsibilities of sustainability. For some this is voluntary; others may feel pressured by advocate demands; for still others it's delegated by a higher business entity.

In terms of being responsible, it's the duty of business as a whole to be stewards of the world. Why? Because collectively, business utilizes the majority of human and economic capital globally. It's also situated upstream from nearly all consumption of resources in the world. With vast resources under its control and a desire for a sustainable future, it's more efficient for business to proactively assume this responsibility than to have all businesses retrofit this duty to the slow, too-little-too-late machinery of governments or the demanding crisis approach of consumer advocate groups.

As organizations work more collaboratively, sustainability responsibilities might also stem from new stakeholder relationships. The responsibility of individuals within businesses also broadens as they adapt a more holistic approach to life balance and fulfillment. This includes increased duty to their communities and beyond, which are a combination of assigned, inherited, and self-imposed responsibilities.

One thing is for sure: What you do with your responsibilities tests your personal and/or organizational mode of conduct.

Once you have a responsibility (or even perceived by others to have a responsibility), you're at choice what you do with it. And your selection will influence the respect, trust, and loyalty of those around you.

You'll find that making good choices results in greater stability for employees, vendors, customers, and other stakeholders and partners. And it showcases your company as a strong leader in the world.

How do you take on such awesome responsibilities? One step at a time, using the principles described in this book. The bonus? Stepping up to the plate will lead to more self-governance now and less governmental and other stakeholder intervention down the road.

THE SYSTAINERSHIP FUNCTION OF IMPARTING STABILITY

In Systainership, imparting stability is the first of the three core functions for building and maintaining a sustainable culture in your company. You build these blocks of stability by shaping them in alliance with relevant stakeholders. The mission, vision, and values that result provide the guiding light for all the other sustainability leadership functions. The stakeholder partnerships, including those involving employees, suppliers, customers, and other organizations, are then carried forward to empower people. And these empowered people permeate the entire organization in compelling and positive ways.

Systainership describes imparting stability as its *first* function because it's an easy, logical place to begin when stepping into the realm of sustainability. See Figure 5. But the entire system is iterative; it's designed for you to revisit this function whenever you use its transparent feedback to do reviews and updates over time.

Systainership™

1.1 Impart Stability

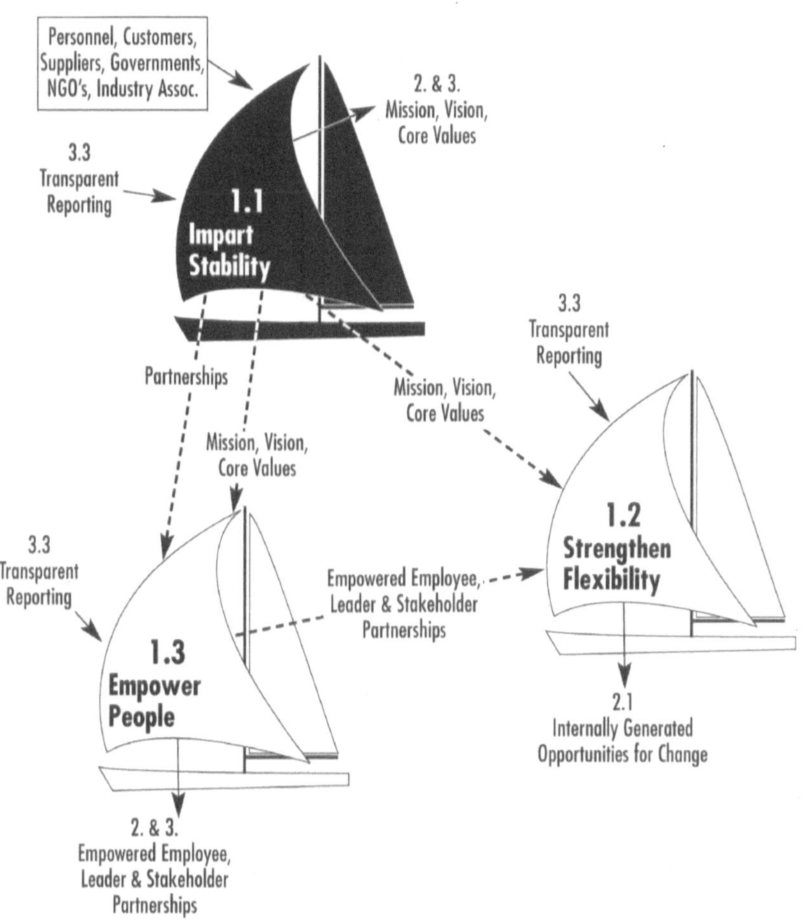

Figure 5

BENEFITS OF SUSTAINABILITY THROUGH IMPARTING STABILITY

Even when everything around you constantly changes, do you realize you can establish many foundational blocks for stakeholders to hang their hats on? Building each of these foundational blocks strengthens the stability—thus the sustainability—of your organization. When people can count on you and your company for what you stand for—to work in collaboration, fulfill your word, and strive for greater stewardship—it provides a sense of security for everyone involved.

Building each of these foundational blocks strengthens the stability—thus the sustainability—of your organization.

These elements of your organizational culture make up the bedrock on which you build solid growth. It will steady your people as they jump hurdles, dismantle barriers, and turn challenges into opportunities—all the while dealing with rapid change. If you use this component of Systainership well, they'll follow you anywhere.

APPLYING SYSTAINERSHIP

Coaching Questions to Move Your Organization Toward Imparting Stability

1. What aspects of sustainability are included in your business vision?
2. What core values are not currently being honored within your business, either explicitly or implicitly?
3. What potential key partnership(s) would immediately benefit your business?

For more coaching questions that will help you lead your business toward greater stability, go to www.SustainableBusinessSystems.com/bq.

Call to Action

Have a meeting with your potential key partners and ask them about their vision and core values. In exchange, they'll likely give you the opportunity to enroll them in what your business is about and the stand it takes.

Your Insights on Imparting Stability

____

____

____

____

____

____

Moving Forward with the Systainership Function of Imparting Stability

What are five steps you can take now to lead your organization toward imparting stability? Please list them in order of priority.

1. ______________________________
2. ______________________________
3. ______________________________
4. ______________________________
5. ______________________________

CHAPTER

6

TRIM THE SAILS WHEN YOU'RE BESIEGED WITH CHANGE

It is not the strongest of the species that survives,
nor the most intelligent,
but the one most responsive to change.

~ CHARLES DARWIN (1809-1882)

Over 200 Years and Thriving—A Lesson from Crane & Co., Inc.

Crane & Co., Inc., an eighth-generation business founded in 1801, has adapted to changes in economics, politics, environment, and technology, and local, national, and world events for more than two centuries.

Its first owner, Zenas Crane, was trained by his father, Stephen, who produced a security paper used by Paul Revere to print notes and help finance the American Revolution.[35] The housewives of Dalton, Massachusetts, provided the company with tough, homemade linen rag that was difficult to turn into pulp but created high-grade paper. From that time forward, the company's mainstay has been high quality, treeless paper.[36] Through all the changes around them, this has remained Crane & Co.'s driving force.

How have Crane & Co.'s leaders maintained the company's strengths while adapting to the changing tides? And how does it continue to thrive in an era that's going paperless?

Few people realize the diversity of this manufacturer of fine stationery, which includes supplying currency paper for the U.S. Treasury, nonwoven materials in circuit boards installed on one of the Apollo missions, components for desalinization plants, smokestack scrubbers, office partitions, and more.[37] Let's look at how this diversity came about.

The company has had several locations, names, and divisions over the years, but for simplification, let's call it Crane. By 1822, mechanization of the paper industry had begun. Zenas Crane invented his own modification to their papermaking machines to retrieve the sheets of paper automatically, rather than by hand. His son, Zenas Marshall Crane, devised a way to incorporate silk threads into paper, which deterred counterfeiting.[38] This made Crane's paper highly desirable to America's new banks.

While transporting paper was a major problem early on, the advent of the railroad in the 1840s opened new markets. In 1851, the company converted an old woolen mill into its first fine writing paper mill. During the Civil War, southern customers refused to pay their northern suppliers and many paper mills went bankrupt. But Crane had devised a method to create paper collars for men, which quickly became fashionable. This short-lived product carried the company through hard times. More important, it led to other stiff-paper applications, which launched its diversification. The company soon produced specialty papers that were turned into machine belts, baskets, washtubs, toboggans, coffins, and even small boats. In 1873, it started producing bullet-patch paper for Winchester rifles.[39]

In 1879, the company again improved its security paper and won the U.S. Treasury bid for producing all of its currency paper.[40] By the turn of the century, their innovations increased the life expectancy of paper bills threefold. Crane then expanded by producing security paper for other countries' banknotes, bonds, stock certificates, and checks. About the same time, it created a thick paper for use in diplomas and certificates, a thin paper for Bibles, and transparent paper for architectural drafting.[41]

When other mills switched to wood pulp and realized significant decreases in operating costs, Crane chose to "stay the course" with its rag-based products.

In 1928, Crane further improved U.S currency paper by embedding scattered red and blue threads. During the depression, the company produced cigarette papers, which led them to developing improved carbon paper—a mainstay product until the advent of computers.[42] During World War II, the company produced war bonds around the clock. Material shortages required using an even higher percentage of cotton than in the pre-war currency paper. The formula changed again in 1951 to take advantage of newer printing processes.[43]

By 1970, the company had introduced several more new paper fibers. In this era, glass and other manmade fibers were used for insulation, filters, and food processing. With the advent of high-quality photocopiers in the 1990s, increased security of currency paper was necessitated once again.[44]

Typically, the contract to produce paper for U.S. currency is put out to bid but, by 1998, Crane had been the U.S. government's sole supplier. The government encouraged others to enter the business, but Crane's continuous innovation kept the U.S. Treasury business in Dalton.[45]

Crane adapted to changing times by asking questions like, "Well, now that this is happening, what can we do?" Its leaders repeatedly came up with solutions under their visionary umbrella of creating high quality, treeless papers. Their eyes stayed open to new markets, new applications, improved processes, adaptive materials, new technologies, and company innovation. Along the way, they have shared their success with their community in Dalton. They led the effort to clean up the Housatonic River, established a research center, and nurtured a culture that excites its workers. Its leaders also kept the company debt low so they could take advantage of new opportunities. According to the company's websites, it's been "green" since day one.[46]

HONING YOUR COMPANY'S FLEXIBILITY

Is your business finding it hard to adapt to today's fast-paced world? Has the machinery of your business become too cumbersome to change? Are your employees set in their ways? Company flexibility is the elasticity that allows your business to bend and not break when the winds of change blow. In fact, being flexible is a critical cultural behavior—an autonomous process that prepares your company for deep change.

> *Company flexibility is the elasticity that allows your business to bend and not break when the winds of change blow.*

Usually, small organizations are inherently more flexible than large ones because they don't have as big a machine that needs to switch gears. Still, flexibility can be honed in any size of organization. The goal is to become capable of continual, crisis-free self-renewal to keep the "change" muscles of your organization exercised. Doing this enables your company to adapt to outside influences as a normal course of business. As you progress, you gain competence by proactively making business development changes that allow you to change ever more quickly. You learn to mix up your leadership style and options to generate new vitality.

Adopting the following 10 practices will assist you in doing exactly that.

10 PRACTICES OF FLEXIBILITY

You can help your company build flexibility to overcome inertia, complacency, and myopia through the 10 leadership practices described here.

1. *Making Change a Process, Not a Goal*

   The popular business fable *Who Moved My Cheese?* by Spencer Johnson, M.D., offers an experiential metaphor for the process of change. It spells out the difference between people being on board with change or not—personified by partner mice Sniff and Scurry (change friendly) and Hem and Haw (not at all!).

Every day they go to the same place in their maze to eat cheese until one day, the cheese isn't there. They are forced to change!

Proactively, Sniff and Scurry set out to explore, finding cheese in new locations at different times while noticing, anticipating, and monitoring what happens so they can enjoy their next meal. Reactively, Hem and Haw resist making change, wishing the cheese would just come back. They want to feel comfortable doing the same thing they always did. But they're so hungry, they're far from comfortable.[47]

While Hem and Haw's only goal was eating their next meal, Sniff and Scurry made change an ongoing process—and enjoyed many wonderful meals.

One thing's for sure: Change keeps happening. You want your leadership to provide the necessary direction so that noticing, anticipating, monitoring, and adapting becomes an automatic process within your organization. Then change is no longer regarded as disruptive. The process becomes ever-present, and the company enjoys flexibility—a quality embraced by people throughout the organization.

2. *Using Your Peripheral View*

Flexibility also comes from paying attention to your surroundings, using a peripheral view as a core competency to minimize surprise. The leaders of Crane & Co. stayed abreast of the opportunities and challenges in the external world. Internally, they looked for opportunities to leverage and adapt their facilities, equipment, processes, products, and management. They also spotted early signs of setbacks.

Today, elements to keep in your peripheral view are more numerous than ever. They include globalization, environmental impacts, proactive stakeholders, and Web 2.0, to name only a few.

Opportunity comes knocking at the door occasionally, but more often it has to be sought out. An opportunity is a change that needs to be fully analyzed and deemed to be on the organization's path to greater sustainability and profitability. Leaders must recognize promising signs and look for the *relationship* of what they see peripherally to the business and its partnerships. Then they must systematically find ways to bring in opportunities they identified while avoiding any crises they see, too.

Large multinational companies have staff dedicated to scanning events within the primary business as well as in the political, technological, and industry publications of other countries where it operates. They constantly look for signs of both problems and opportunities. Small companies tend to ask employees, industry scouts, teams tracking developments, customer watchdogs, social network trend spotters, and others to assist. The smallest organizations can at least have a suggestion box and reward people for any ideas the company takes into action.

Companies of all sizes are wise to use this peripheral view concept to discover and illuminate the "inconceivable."

3. *Behaving Proactively*

Once you've found your peripheral view, examining potential crises and untapped opportunities follows. When a crisis arises, putting your head in the sand and hoping it will go away can lead to disaster. So can turning your back on newfound opportunities due to the fear of managing too much change. Being proactive at the first signs of either puts you in the seat of command, empowering you to come up with well-planned strategies.

Yes, opportunities create new frontiers, career paths, technologies, markets, and inventions. By *not* being proactive, you run the risk of later having to react to short-term crises in ways that could compromise long-term benefits.

As an example, let's consider the opportunity to become a sustainable business with triple-based profitability. Many businesses are proactively adopting this choice as you'll see in the examples throughout this book. These businesses have a compelling, sustainable vision and work to reap the benefits over time.

Some companies wait for new government regulations to force compliance in new areas of environmental or social stewardship. Their leaders believe the playing field will be leveled *for all* if everyone is required to comply. But by waiting, they might be forced to retrofit their operations to meet environmental or other compliance requirements at great expense, including costly monitoring and enforcement. At best, these efforts are "doing less bad."

If you wait for new sustainability regulations, you could find yourself in the same boat. However, behaving proactively gives you the flexibility to design sustainable practices that strategically fit your business, nurture its profitability, and contribute to a more sustainable business model. By acting now, you'd save on expensive retrofitting while reaping numerous benefits including longevity. Behaving proactively reflects the depth of your commitment to the sustainability of your organization. In contrast, operating in *reactionary* ways can severely limit future possibilities for your company.

For more than 200 years, Crane & Co. recognized opportunities and introduced new products but remained true to the main direction of the business. Savvy business leaders also recognize when to say "no" to an opportunity that's not in complete alignment with the company's core strengths and mission—as Crane did with the advent of wood pulp. (Chapter 11 discusses how to create these alignments.)

4. *Recognizing Stagnancy and Strategic Paralysis*

   Within an organization, stagnancy and strategic paralysis can be found many places and at many levels. Signs include nonperforming bottom lines, low employee morale, shelved strategic plans, lack of communication, strong resistance to change, not identifying opportunities, closed-minded management, or constant plan reviews.

   Be on the lookout for stagnant entities in which everyone has become too comfortable doing the same thing the same way. It can suck the life out of that business function! Marching in place makes any organization rigid over time. When change occurs, stagnant parts of the organization can't overcome the inertia and respond in a timely manner. Clearly, this lack of ability to go with the flow severely hampers a business's opportunities.

What can be done? You can exercise your change muscles.

5. *Exercising the Change Muscles*

Like physical muscles, the biceps of business must be stretched, flexed, strengthened, and relaxed so your organization can be more resilient when needed. Exercise also creates new energy, dedication, and motivation—all leading to new developments.

You can exercise organizational change muscles by questioning well-established assumptions and creating activities around doing so in any business segment. Test your assumptions using today's parameters to see if they hold true. If they don't, let them go! Develop new operational guidelines in the affected business areas, replacing these limiting beliefs with innovative ways to do business that employees are eager to adopt.

Like physical muscles, the biceps of business must be stretched, flexed, strengthened, and relaxed so your organization can be more resilient when needed.

According to Paul J. H. Shoemaker and Robert E. Gunther writing in the June 2006 *Harvard Business Review*, another way to exercise change muscles is making intentional mistakes that are *good* for your organization.

Yes, mistakes can be costly, but Shoemaker and Gunther in *The Wisdom of Deliberate Mistakes* say it's all in the timing. "Research shows that executives who apply a conventional, systematic approach to solving a pattern recognition problem are often slower to find the solution than those who test their assumptions by knowingly making mistakes."

When is the timing right? When you become perplexed by complex problems and the potential learning from a failure exceeds its potential expense. Learning faster than your rivals is a strategic advantage. So realize that failing often, fast, and inexpensively may just give you the lead in your industry.[48]

For young businesses, both Gifford Pinchot III, author of *Intrapreneur*, and Jill Bamberg, author of *Getting to Scale*, guide you to morph your business plan early on and frequently. Pinchot impressed upon Bamberg that "faster learning beats better planning." Organic Valley Family of Farms started in produce but found its ultimate niche in the dairy industry.[49] Zappos.com started as a shoe retailer and now is an online marketer of many retail lines. You can see how Crane & Co. morphed over several generations.

What's the theory behind this morphing? The early learning experience from each transformation is more valuable than spending your start-up years on extensive planning on a single track. It broadens your base of experience from which to focus your business, and it puts the business in the habit of staying flexible. For well-established companies, this could be done on a small scale throughout the organization, especially when unexpected opportunities arise.

Like any exercise routine, getting started is hard. But after you diligently lead your company to exercise its change muscles, you'll get over the "wall," and it becomes routine practice.

6. *Leveraging Synchronicity*

Have you ever noticed what happens once you become fully committed to a path? Suddenly, resources and opportunities arrive from out of the blue with an ease you couldn't have imagined.

In my own life, I saw how commitment activates synchronicity like magic. When my husband and I *committed* to move to Hawaii in 2004, we developed a strategy, took action, and the magic appeared! Amazingly, we sold our house in just six weeks and purchased airline flights to Hawaii that had just gone on sale. Our friends rallied with all kinds of assistance that included—

- providing interim accommodations after selling the house.

- managing the moving company to containerize our belongings in storage.
- hosting a going-away luau so we could say good-bye to friends we left behind.
- transporting us from the shipping docks (where we left our vehicles for ocean passage) to a hotel and the airport the next day.
- finding guest quarters to rent in Hawaii until we located our new home.

In addition, the second house we looked at in Hawaii fit *exactly* what we had envisioned. Our good fortune continued. Without realizing it, we had created such a strong vision and passion for our life in Hawaii that when we got committed and communicated with our friends, they eagerly helped us make it happen.

As humans, when something synchronistic pops up, we either recognize it and seize it, or we let it go and miss the opportunity. In his book *Synchronicity: The Inner Path of Leadership*, Joseph Jaworski states that the power of synchronicity shouldn't surprise us. Once we are totally committed, we see the world as being fundamentally *connected* instead of fragmented happenings. The challenge becomes finding reasons to connect them.

Once we are totally committed, we see the world as being fundamentally connected *instead of fragmented happenings.*

Do you see how leaders in a flexible organization hone their ability to recognize synchronous events, strategies, resources, stakeholder alignments, and more? They look for the *relatedness* between such things rather than the things themselves.

Being committed provides a fresh perspective for seeing what's already there but wasn't recognized. It can add determination to seizing new opportunities. Looking at synchronicity this way might tarnish the sense of magic, but it makes us realize its power and creates a more authentic and inclusive path to success.

7. *Adopting a Learner Attitude*

Are your employees fearful of change? Do they resist taking responsibility for their own actions and thoughts? Are they judgmental and biased? Do they seem to know it all? Do they lobby to place themselves in a winning position?

If so, introducing a "learner" behavior could greatly benefit your company. How? By fostering the power of curiosity and relating it in a win-win way. It precludes judgments that come from close-minded positions—from people thinking they already know the answer to a problem.

Having a learner attitude removes us from our own biases, beliefs, and opinions; we act like questioning researchers or reporters delving into the essential business truth. It develops a deep curiosity, which yields creativity and solutions instead of placing blame. With this attitude in place, you see how to create winning outcomes for all while being more accepting of others—even those in judgment, yourself included. In addition, it yields to greater inclusivity than ever when finding solutions.

Having a learner attitude removes us from our own biases, beliefs, and opinions; we act like questioning researchers or reporters delving into the essential business truth.

The learner mode works best when you employ open-ended questions—finding out the who, what, where, when, and how of a situation. You'll notice that the question "why" is omitted. Although "why" is an open-ended question, it's often regarded as confrontational and meets with resistance. Asking closed questions—those that can be answered "yes" or "no"—doesn't open conversations to more information and isn't as useful.

To foster a learner mindset in your organization, lead by example with your associates. Help them adopt this attitude and express their curiosity using open-ended questions. In *Competing for the Future*, Gary Hamel and C. K. Prahalad suggest your goal be to develop deep and boundless curiosity. This book lists many strategic open-ended questions that top managers of large, well-known U.S. companies are asking themselves to learn how they might pursue major industry trends. For example, they ask, "How do we want our industry to be shaped in five to ten years?" or "What will be the basis for our competitive advantage in the future?"[50] You're wise to model questions like these as you pursue your own company issues.

This open-minded approach increases flexibility within your organization and can be used at any and all levels. Your employees will be seen as open, receptive, and flexible rather than rigid, close-minded, and judgmental. Indeed, the information gleaned will enhance the sustainability of your organization by—

- challenging assumptions.
- exploring new possibilities.
- setting up greater learning.
- minimizing confrontations.
- creating new awareness.
- fostering innovation.

Flexibility allows you to look at problems and solutions through multiple, well-researched perspectives. When you combine this explorative mindset with a sustainability lens for examining your challenges and opportunities, a whole new world opens. (Chapter 11 explores the sustainability lens concept further.)

8. *Collaborating Across Organizational Lines*

Historically, organizations have been organized bureaucratically within a hierarchy based on authority and command. The resulting silos of business create walls that are difficult to penetrate. Then in the 1980s, companies started to organize around functions, divisions, and a combination of both known as "matrix." It's also when decision-making moved toward discussion and developing consensus.

Here are three newer organizational styles based on strategy and business purpose with collaboration, alliance, and synergy as their focus:

- Team structure – success depends on all its teams (e.g., Whole Foods)

- Network structure – contracts out major functions of its operations and then coordinates and controls resulting relationships (e.g., Patagonia)
- Virtual structure – manages all company alliances in cyberspace (e.g., eBay's WorldofGood.com)

Given that each structure has its strengths and weaknesses, it's important to set up your organization in a way that suits your business needs.

But with any organizational structure, you can break down limiting walls and encourage collaboration and synergy by developing special-purpose, cross-disciplinary teams. For example, a hierarchical organization might create a team to promote a new product line. The team could consist of members from finance, marketing, product development, sales, production, distribution, R&D, IT, and so on. It could also involve others including artists, environmental specialists, community developers, and educators.

Such cross-disciplinary teams bring a variety of perspectives to the purpose at hand, thus enhancing both the flexibility and sustainability of the products being developed. This system of checks and balances can maximize the use of valuable resources in the long run. The ideas generated from cross-disciplinary teams tend to have immediate buy-in across the organization, with communications led by the team members. Plus these teams don't have the complicated management issues that are common in permanent matrix organizations.

In small companies where employees and resources are already stretched to the limit, "virtual" teams of employees and other stakeholders could be encouraged to collaborate by asking them to comment on new product ideas, perhaps as part of an incentive program.

Another scenario might be creating functional teams in a team-structured organization. For example, in difficult economic times, your company might benefit from forming a team of finance experts pulled from teams throughout the company to examine the best funding practices for the times.

The benefits are clear. Creating and realigning project teams as organizational needs change keep the company and employees nimble while leveraging the expertise at hand.

9. *Leveraging the Power of Your Resources*
   Even if you don't think of resources as being powerful, realize that anything in great quantity, size, efficiency, or weight carries power. Case in point is the historical power the oil industry has wielded over governments and auto manufacturers. And look at the power the New York Stock Exchange has on commodity pricing. In an event-based example, China showcased its primary national resource—its population of more than one billion—to the world in the opening and closing ceremonies of the 2008 Beijing Summer Olympics. The choreography featuring 2008 dancers awed the world and showed how pooled resources could deliver a unified result.

   But how do small-to-medium-sized businesses leverage their resources?

   First, consider the effects of "renewable versus nonrenewable" resources on your business. Ask where can you convert more of the "nonrenewable" to "renewable," then find areas where you can pool resources and get double duty from existing resources. (Crane & Co. has provided several clear examples of this.)

   You can start by borrowing ideas from other models such as permaculture. One design principle of the permaculture approach is for individual elements to perform multiple functions—for example, having an office building with garden roofs. That way, a plot of land becomes multipurpose as a building site with a garden, while the garden itself is multipurpose because it keeps the building cooler and lowers energy needs. It also provides "people" food, "bee" food, and perhaps flowers for commercial sale.

   Opportunities for leveraging resources can also come from partnering with nonprofits and ensuring each organization benefits from pooling your resources. When manufacturing firms partner with a nonprofit organizations to test-market new products or provide training in underserved communities, resources from all three partners come together for the benefit of each. For example, HP partners with the United Nations Industrial Development Organization (UNIDO) to implement its Graduate Entrepreneurship Training through IT (GET-IT) program in Africa and other regions of the world. They provide IT training to young people, which makes them eligible for jobs, which helps grow the local economy, which will eventually create new markets for HP.

You can also leverage your people resources. Chapter 7 talked about how to empower your employees through aligning personal vision, skills, and talents with the company's mission, vision, and needs. When considering leveraging resources, this could lead to a person doing more than one job type in the traditional sense—an excellent small business approach. You might find someone in marketing with skills as a "sleuth reporter" who can seek out opportunities that need to be brought to management's attention. Or, perhaps you might discover one of your warehouse receivers is skilled in graphic design. Clearly, you can tap into employee skill sets like these and let them do what they do well.

10. *Identifying and Engaging Sustainability Advocates*

Across your organization you'll find certain employees who have aligned themselves—personally, professionally, or both—with environmental and social stewardship. These sustainability advocates promote practices for increasing social and environmental stewardship as they deem practical within their current position. The more exuberant of these advocates champion their efforts using existing communication channels. Identify these advocates; they're born leaders who want to inspire others. Empower them with acceptance and define their new role within the organization. They've already shown their eagerness to participate in a new world design. By engaging these advocates, you're gaining new perspective on how your company can become part of that effort!

Bringing your sustainability advocates together also helps you pursue the sustainability of your business. They've shown a passion that's not yet realized in other employees. You can put them into a special-purpose, cross-disciplinary team and provide them with organizational support. Then they'll develop new strategies and business cases to make sustainable changes that are relevant to your business. While this group helps you expand your company's sustainability and flexibility, it also feeds opportunities and challenges into your business analysis. This can be an excellent source for developing or expanding your sustainable business model.

In small companies, people resources are more limited than in large companies. However, you'll see fresh energy generated when you recognize these advocates and charge them with responsibilities they genuinely care about. This will motivate them to find new ways to increase productivity and free some of their time to work in new areas of sustainability.

SYSTAINERSHIP FUNCTION OF STRENGTHENING FLEXIBILITY

Using this leadership function of Systainership, be sure to bring together empowered employees, managers, and stakeholder partners to build in flexibility as a fundamental behavior of your organization. This function generates well-thought-out avenues of change that develop the adaptability needed for your business to evolve. The feasibility of implementing such changes is evaluated from a holistic perspective in the Systainership function of maintaining a steady focus at the helm, described in Chapter 9. In turn, this strengthens your company's ability to absorb opportunities for generating triple-based profitability. See Figure 6.

Systainership™

1.2 Strengthen Flexibility

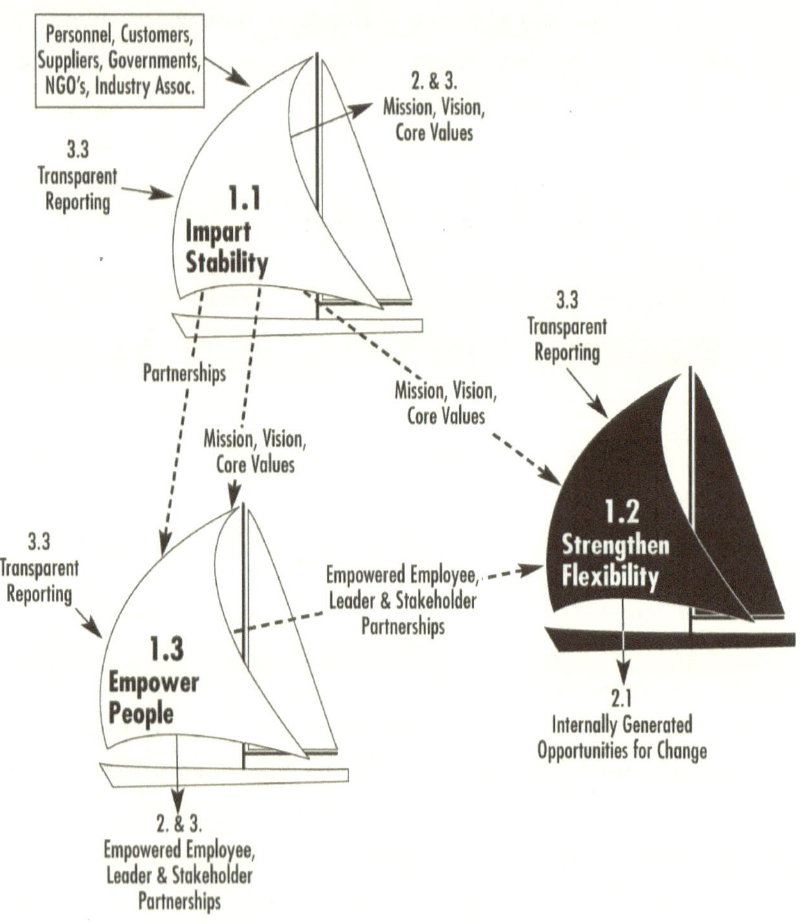

Figure 6

SUSTAINABILITY BENEFITS THROUGH STRENGTHENING FLEXIBILITY

In summary, being flexible increases the sustainability of your organization. How? By allowing your company to bounce back from adversity and thrust forward toward new horizons. It also keeps you on a sustainable track by transforming the fear of change into a powerful mechanism for embracing change autonomously.

To leverage these efforts to their fullest, make sure your organization operates in complete alignment with its vision and mission. Energy from that alignment makes it possible to naturally adopt the flexibility practices noted in this chapter. After that, honing them becomes much easier.

APPLYING SYSTAINERSHIP

Coaching Questions to Move Your Organization Toward Strengthening Flexibility

1. Which of the 10 flexibility practices, if implemented, would have the greatest impact on the sustainability of your organization, enabling it to operate more successfully in a fast-changing world?
2. Who would be your key players for implementing this practice?
3. What would it take to fully integrate this practice into your business operations?

For more coaching questions to help your business become more flexible, go to www.SustainableBusinessSystems.com/bq.

Call to Action

Meet with your key players and enroll them in establishing this greater flexibility.

Your Insights on Strengthening Flexibility

____

____

____

____

____

____

Moving Forward with the Systainership Function of Strengthening Flexibility

What are five steps you can take now to lead your organization toward strengthening flexibility? Please list them in order of priority.

1. ____
2. ____
3. ____
4. ____
5. ____

CHAPTER

7

EMPOWER PEOPLE AND CULTIVATE NEW ENERGY

Individual commitment to a group effort—that is what makes a team work, a company work, a society work, a civilization work.

~ VINCE LOMBARDI (1913-1970)

"Family" Culture Gives New Life— A Lesson from Hamakua Springs Country Farms

Hamakua Springs Country Farms is a company that was given a second life due to innovative ideas from its workers. In 2008, these dedicated employees, laboring hard as banana crop growers and pickers for an average of $12 an hour, came up with a plan to keep the farm alive.

Richard Ha had founded this 600-acre banana and vegetable farm on the northeast coast of Hawaii's Big Island in 1973. He was distressed by shrinking profits from rising fertilizer and energy costs, re-occurrences of a banana crop virus, competition from Central America, stagnant market prices, and the challenge of finding enough workers to tend the fields.[51]

Ha and his family deliberated hard before deciding to shut down the banana operation. In early April, Ha announced the closure to his workers. The following Monday, the workers showed up and met with Ha to present a plan for saving the operation. *They figured out how to run it with fewer workers while increasing production by nearly 10% an acre.*

Upon further analysis, Ha realized his competition—companies that imported bananas—would soon have to raise their prices due to the increased price of oil and the weak U.S. dollar.[52] He also considered that his company would soon realize energy savings from a hydroelectric installation on the farm. So Ha and his family reversed their decision to close and continued shipping bananas from Hamakua Farms to all the Hawaiian islands using the new plan.

What motivated these employees to take action? Ha explained this at the 2008 Kuleana Green Business Conference on the Big Island of Hawaii. He said his employees are like ʻohana (family): "We are family and take care of each other as best we can." For years, Ha and his related family had been using their creativity to help their employees as best they could. Due to rising costs and stagnant prices, the Ha family couldn't raise wages to assist the workers with their increasing cost of living. Instead, they helped them in other ways. Employee compensation, in addition to the hourly wage, included full health benefits and lots of free fruits and vegetables from the farm to ease the hardships of a tough economy. Even the laid-off workers were given produce every week.

Their creative efforts to help employees will get even better. With their hydroelectric project, Ha will provide plug-in recharging for hybrid cars. The company also plans to produce its own biodiesel fuel for farm equipment and other vehicles, setting the goal of being energy self-sufficient. That means to reduce commuting costs, employees will be able to either plug in or fill up with biodiesel fuel. They also plan to create a pond for raising shrimp and fish for the workers because they'll have their own power to recycle the water back into their system. In addition, they'll raise pigs, feeding them banana and tomato waste, and smoke their meat to supplement the workers' diet.

All these efforts help build employee loyalty as well as provide support for the whole community.

Clearly, the employees of Hamakua Springs Country Farms wanted to keep their jobs and summoned fresh energy around a new business plan. That, in turn, motivated their employer. Their initiative pays homage to the ‘ohana culture while being the driving force for the owners to keep the workers employed *and* provide food for Hawaiians. “They really wanted to make it happen. They said they would work hard. I felt I had to meet their commitment,” said Ha.[53]

---

12 WAYS TO EMPOWER PEOPLE AND CULTIVATE NEW ENERGY

Is your company suffering from high turnover rates? Are your employees more apt to say “That’s not my responsibility” than to say “I did it because it needed to be done”? Empowering employees transfers power to them to become idea generators, problem solvers, and decision makers like the workers of Hamakua Springs Country Farms.

Here are 12 ways you can empower your employees and other stakeholders to work collaboratively toward your organization’s goals.

1. *Look at Individual Capacities Versus Human Resources*
   Leaders can no longer look at their employees as a collective human resource. Each employee is a unique human being with a contribution to make. Traditionally, business leaders have gotten things done by exercising control and authority, simply by being in command. But dangling the proverbial carrot in front of employees is no longer effective. Cultural changes in the last two decades have left people wanting more control in their own lives *and* a sense of fulfillment. For example, Generation Y employees want more than a job, more than a paycheck; they want to feel part of the solution to the success of your business.

The concept of partnering, introduced in Chapter 5, encourages you to partner with your employees and other associates. You can take the lead to align their values, purpose, and passions with those of your company, which means advocating ways to apply each individual's strengths where they're best used. Ask yourself, "How can my company co-create employee positions to realize a higher value for everyone involved?"

2. *Understand and Use Emotional Intelligence (EI)*

Emotional intelligence (EI) refers to the ability to recognize, assess, and manage the emotions of individuals, teams, and oneself. The definition of EI has been evolving since first introduced by Darwin. Psychiatrist and contemporary thought leader Daniel Goleman defines EI as a set of skills related to how one communicates, interacts, and manages feelings. He believes that EI can be more important than IQ—or even more important than the specific skills and knowledge required to be a top-performing leader of any company, from a Fortune 500 to any small business or nonprofit.[54] Indeed, EI contributed to Ha's employees' desire to help him find solutions rather than close down.

Overall, EI research conveys the importance of interweaving these "soft" talents into other leadership empowerment practices to achieve better business results.

3. *Leverage Your Influence*

Webster's dictionary lists the primary definition of a leader as "one who guides on the way, especially by going in advance."

How do leaders do this? Through their influence, they somehow affect the choices of others. That suggests that influence is the essence of true leadership and also that everyone can lead. After all, in everything you do and say, consciously or not, you influence those around you. Often your circle of influence is larger than you might realize. Know that the strength of your influence, though, is affected by the alignment of your purpose and values. What

... in everything you do and say, consciously or not, you influence those around you.

methods can you use to strengthen your ability to influence others?

You can apply this principle of leveraging your influence to any leadership model. Here are a few examples of the many leadership models available:

- In Hawaii, Rosa Say's Managing with Aloha has become well known.
- Kaplan and Norton have created the Balanced Scorecard methodology.
- Charles Knight, CEO of Emerson Electric, Best Buy stores, Stephen Covey, and John Cotter all tout their own styles and methods of leadership.

Leaders determine the best model for their business. No matter which method you practice, how you influence others sets up your leadership effectiveness—not only by what you *do* and *say*, but by *how you say it.*

Do you think influencing is done proactively to persuade or sway others on a conscious level? Not always. Your unconscious actions, moods, and tones also wield quite an impact as the scenarios that follow show.

Imagine a VP of marketing strutting into the office with a "Good morning! Ready for the weekly status meeting?" But with his tie hanging out of his pocket, he hardly looks ready. Then he delays the start to go into his office and search through stacks of files to find his reports. Finally, he comes back and opens the meeting by asking, "Our sales were down 3% last month. Who's not pulling their weight?"

Rewind. Here's a new take: A neatly groomed VP of marketing walks into the meeting five minutes ahead of its scheduled time. He greets everyone personally and genuinely with good humor, picks up the sales file prepared by his assistant, and seats himself in the conference room ready to start on time. He begins by asking, "Our sales appear to be down 3% for last month. What factors should we look at to learn what might have influenced this?"

Both VPs are leading by example, but which one would you want to work for and support? Which one motivates you? Now look in the mirror and realize how what *you* say can influence others. Are your words positive, negative, stagnant, or what?

Consciously strive to be aware of the influence you have and want. Use this power to bring about behaviors that lead to desired results. Reach out and help others change their behaviors so they'll work smarter, be more productive, and achieve greater success than ever before.

4. *Empower Yourself*

How you empower *yourself* reflects how you affect those in your sphere of influence. Remember occasions when you saw others act so energetically and enthusiastically about their work that you thought, "Gee, I wish I had some of that"?

People who enjoy their work have a clear vision that aligns with their individual purpose, values, and passions. They work from their strengths, overcome obstacles, do more with less stress, and strive to live their potential. Follow this lead by influencing *yourself* in these empowering ways. Become a leader in your own life!

As a powerful self leader, you have the ability to enroll others. When you do, your employees will want the excitement and enthusiasm you show. What will they be saying about you? How piqued will their interest be in working with you?

This all requires nurturing personal relationships to achieve positive outcomes. Don't look at your employees as a collective human resource. Rather, regard each one as the unique embodiment of his or her potential. Then capitalize on this potential by executing the empowerment practices in this book.

5. *Tap into the Expertise of Others*

If you want to pursue excellence within your organization, consider forming your own executive team. Chapter 5 addressed two approaches—developing partnerships and forming cross-disciplinary teams. You can extend these to your own executive team.

Why include executives from the various functional divisions of your organization? It will help you—

- permeate any organizational walls that exist.
- employ appropriate change management practices where needed.
- pinpoint blind spots.
- reveal opportunities and challenges through the sustainability lens, especially if the executives are known champions of the sustainability effort.

Forming this kind of an SEC (Sustainability/Executive/Change Management) team lets you also brainstorm the overarching direction and strategies for business as you draw on the perspectives of multiple disciplines, divisions, and locations. Remember, each team member excels when he or she aligns with the mission, vision, values, and sustainability objectives of the organization. The SEC team works under your direction to collaborate on organizational directives. For example, Richard Ha's team, though not an executive team, executed this approach expertly to benefit all.

As a leader, you may occasionally feel alone at the top, even with an SEC team in place. How can you get objective input from within your own company? Often you can't, so many leaders turn to an external mastermind group. In it, participants feel free to challenge each other, to raise the bar higher than ever. They feel free to support each other with genuine honesty, respect, and compassion. These peers don't feel apprehensive about giving you feedback. In fact, they'll give you fresh perspectives from outside your business or industry. Often they contribute solutions to issues you might not have noticed within the "box" of your own organization.

Through their support, SEC teams and mastermind groups further empower leaders. They draw on a breadth of experience while providing a sounding board and generating new ideas. Indeed, they're among the best ways you can create synergy at the leadership level.

6. *Develop a Clear, Concise, and Sustainable Business Model*

Your business model describes how your organization creates, delivers, and captures economic, social, environmental, or other forms of value. It's derived from your organization's mission, vision, and strengths.

Use your model to spell out your organization's offerings, policies, structure, product lines, markets, resource strategies, operating procedures, and means of trade. If done well, your model makes it clear to everyone *what* your company does, *why* it does it, and *how* it does it. Each component should further contribute to the sustainability of your business. For example, after Richard Ha and his employees revisited the farm business model, they took out elements they had once thought were sustainable and proved not to be, thus strengthening the model.

No matter how many incandescent light bulbs you replace, how much water you conserve, or how well you take care of your employees, if your business is based on scarce fossil fuels, heavy metals, or non-regenerative natural resources and company practices don't change, your business's longevity is in question. So is the amount of impact it can have on the world.

Many more factors affect sustainability. To identify them as you create a sustainable business model, examine tools such as The Natural Step, Cradle to Cradle, ISO 14000, the Australian Ecologically Sustainable Development Process, and others. Some of these are described briefly in Chapter 11.

Today organizations are asking the tough questions that affect the core of their identity.

Today organizations are asking the tough questions that affect the core of their identity. Here are just a few examples:

- Interface, Inc.: How can carpet be manufactured without substances derived from fossil fuels?
- Nike: How can we produce our athletic shoes more sustainably?
- State of Hawaii 2050 sustainability plan: How can this state be sustainable in all walks of life and industry?

Confronting questions like these is critical for these entities to survive in the long term—and the answers to such questions can provide the guiding star for your business. You might even incorporate this guiding star into your company vision and operational strategies. Your challenge is to determine which sustainability strategy is most appropriate right now to grow and sustain your business. (Chapter 11 delves into criteria for sustainability under the topic of strategy alignment.)

Defining your market is key to producing a *sustainable* business model—that is, what you do, who you do it for, and why you do it. Even if you have fabulous ideas for products or services, the sustainability of your market must be determined early in the process of developing your model.

Some companies believe being "green" will answer their marketing woes. But nothing beats good old-fashioned legwork to acquire all the background information on your market and make solid projections to analyze its potential.

For example, a company may be enamored with the whole concept of installing photovoltaic systems for generating renewable energy. Perhaps company leaders even decided between residential and commercial installations. But what is the potential for this market in the area they've chosen to do business? Who are their competitors? How will they differentiate themselves? How easy is it for others to enter this market? What do they see as the lifespan of the market? Do they want to adapt beyond that? Ask these questions!

Understand that no perfect, uncontested market exists, but that doesn't mean you shouldn't try to position your business in the strongest market possible. Your business model might be strong in all other areas, but operating in a shaky market will cause your business to struggle and even shorten its lifespan.

7. *Establish Transparent Communication*

Communicating transparently has such wide implications that a separate chapter—Chapter 16—has been devoted to it. Just know that the communication of accurate, trustworthy organizational information empowers all relationships, both internal and external. Open communication conveys not only good results and opportunities, it also confronts the challenges encountered along the way.

Stakeholders feel more enabled when they have relevant, accurate, and sufficient information to work from. They'll get fully engaged with your organization when they're trusted with relevant knowledge and data. (Chapter 12 discusses how to establish trustworthy, relevant data.)

8. *Create Intention*

Doing an activity *with intention* means executing it with commitment and resolve.

The intention of a business model with its resulting operations, practices, and procedures is driven by a commitment to the company's mission, vision, and values as well as its strategies to achieve them. Successful strategies and practices are those each employee can recite while showing how his or her job contributes to achieving the overall vision. This way, the entire organization works as a cohesive unit. Everyone shares the drive, passion, and engagement as they align with the objectives of the organization. Employees become engaged with their work on multiple levels—physically, mentally, emotionally, and even spiritually in the sense of being aligned with their purpose in life. The power inherent in this engagement creates positive, high-intensity energy, which cultivates even greater commitment and resolve.

So be bold with your intentions! As Goethe wisely said, "Whatever you can do, or dream you can, begin it. Boldness has genius, power and magic in it."

9. *Play to Everyone's Strengths*

Marcus Buckingham, in conjunction with the Gallup Organization, has extensively researched how to draw the greatest potential from employees and written several books on this subject. The Gallup® Strengths-Based Organization model is used at Interface[55] and other companies.[56] Buckingham's findings show that putting employees in the "right" position based on their core strengths is more important than matching their skills and knowledge to the job. He defines core strengths as inbred talents that can't be taught. Yes, skills can be gained through experience and knowledge can be acquired through education. But if an employee's inbred talents line up for a particular position, then the corresponding skills and education can come with time.[57]

The old-style philosophy promoted the idea of obtaining additional training in talent weaknesses to improve productivity efficiency, and effectiveness on the job. Buckingham has shown that, at best, this results is marginal improvements and suggests it's better to improve productivity, efficiency, and effectiveness by honing one's core strengths.[58]

More than that, when people work from their strengths, they feel good about themselves. Specifically, they feel empowered to carry out their responsibilities and get excited about improving on those strengths.

Realize that a strength doesn't measure how well people will perform their jobs. Rather, it indicates how they go about doing a job *well.* People with different core strengths can do a job equally well but in different ways. Some strengths align better with particular jobs, and this can be taken into consideration when placing employees. In an ideal world, jobs would be defined based on a careful alignment of employee strengths and organizational needs. In a less-than-ideal world, a close alignment becomes the goal.

One way to achieve this in teams is to chart the strengths of each team member and aggregate them to determine which ones might be lacking to meet the team's goals. This helps determine who might complement existing strengths and sets up the team to work together effectively. Understanding each other's strengths enhances collaborative work throughout the organization.

Organizational strengths are also important. Some are inherent in its nature, but many are acquired over the years and are unique to every company. These are the strengths highlighted in the traditional SWOT (Strengths, Weakness, Opportunities,

Threats) analysis and include the attributes of the company that are helpful in achieving its vision. Examples of organizational strengths include having—

- a low debt equity ratio.
- an international distribution system in place.
- strong community support.

Just as employee strengths are considered when positioning people in their jobs, organizational strengths are considered when selecting appropriate strategies.

Ideally, a strengths-based organization aligns the core strengths of its employees and its organizational strengths. This generates power all around, building confidence and competence while generating accountability. The effects can be as far-reaching as improved productivity, increased profits, greater customer satisfaction, and lower turnover.

10. Make Work Play

The concept of making work play is difficult for many to grasp. When I was asked more than 20 years ago how my work could seem like play, I couldn't fathom there was even an answer. It was ingrained in me from childhood that "work is work and play is play." Also, at the time, my work fell so far out of alignment with who I was as a person, I couldn't even comprehend the idea. It didn't fit into the box that defined my world.

Years later, I discovered the answer when I realized I could redefine the paradigm of my world. Today, I joyously work in a profession I love, in an arena for which I have great passion, and in a way that brings me fulfillment and balance with the lifestyle I want while providing great value to my business and customers.

What's the key? Personal alignment. That is, when employees align their personal mission, vision for the future, deeply held values, core strengths, genius, and passions with the work they do, they experience the sheer pleasure of full engagement. They discover freedom from personal conflict and the power of a unified existence. Without this, they have internal conflict and stress; they lack dedication, motivation, and proficiency.

Alignment of strengths—one aspect of personal alignment listed earlier—is a great place to start bringing joy into your work. It's where I start with each executive I coach. This easy tool can be used immediately to help you create other leadership tools in your box.

Aligning the vision and mission of an individual to those of an organization is the first litmus test for a strong employee relationship. The degree of alignment is based on how much overlap exists. Once the individual and company leaders determine how their missions and visions can be mutually realized, then it's worth pursuing what an employee/company partnership could look like.

Aligning the vision and mission of an individual to those of an organization is the first litmus test for a strong employee relationship.

The next level of exploration considers the alignment of employee and organizational values, core strengths, genius, and passion. Again, a perfect match isn't necessary, just the ability to pursue one within the other to benefit both. Compare Figures 7a and 7b to see an example of how personal and business values and visions can align.

This concept of alignment extends well beyond employee applications. Investment firms are aligning with the core values of their investors; "green" companies are aligning with the core values and purposes of their customers. Similarly, you can look for ways to leverage alignment as an empowerment tool in multiple arenas of your business and your life.

11. *Lead the Charge into New Frontiers and a New World Design*

What attracts the attention of upcoming generations like those in Generation Y? Companies that step out on the edge of new

Systainership™

Sample Alignment of Personal and Business Values and Visions

Personal Profile

Purpose: To generate health and wellness in the world.

Passions:

- Being vibrant, energized and in good health: physically, mentally and emotionally active
- Having an extraordinary relationship with my family
- A holistic *application of my pharmaceutical laboratory skills*
- *Feeling spiritually connected and one with the world*
- Having thriving friendships full of stimulation and fun

Values: *Integrity*, Freedom of Choice, *Being my Best, Empowering Others*, Variety/ Change of Pace

Core Strengths: Achiever, *Strategic*, Relator, Responsibility, *Futuristic*

Genius: Solving Puzzles

Personal Vision:
I use my talents and skills in *partnership* with loved ones and business associates giving me the career that I love, giving me loving, intimate relationships, and supporting myself to be the best I can be in all that I do, believe, and extend to the world.

Mission:
To use my experience and sense of adventure to help others *realize healthier and more fulfilling lives.*

Note: *Italicized type* highlights areas of alignment.

Figure 7a

Systainership™

Sample Alignment of Personal and Business Values and Visions

Business Profile

Business Mission:
Bringing *meaningful improvement to the lives of people around the world living at risk with widespread, life-threatening illnesses.*

Core Business Values:
Integrity, Partnership, Delivering Value-added to Customers, *Innovation, Use of Strengths,* Self-Leadership, *Empowerment*

Business Vision:
Working *strategically* in *collaboration with local partners* to convert and commercialize high-value novel *pharmaceuticals* for the mass markets of developing countries.

Note: *Italicized type* highlights areas of alignment.

Figure 7b

product, technology, and market frontiers with greater inclusivity to create a more sustainable world. These young people are coming out of the chute technology ready, ecologically minded, and concerned with societal challenges. Many in Generation Y won't even look for a job with a company that doesn't demonstrate sustainable business practices.

Many companies have stepped forward to be industry leaders in creating sustainability. Interface, Inc. comes to mind as the first major corporation in this arena with the lists of other companies growing. For example, the B-Corp List—a list of companies certified by the non-profit B-Lab to "use the power of business to solve social and environmental problems"—includes more than 430 companies.[59]

Looking ahead, some industries will be reconfigured to make their products sustainable. Whole new industries will be launched to replace those that cannot be reconfigured. It's becoming a new age of innovation, a time when the sustainability of globalizing commerce is being questioned and a period to unify the world with common goals.

In leading your company, you'll be required to set the course for the future, navigate around the obstacles, and lead with clarity and commitment toward a sustainable future. You have a big but exciting job. By empowering others, you'll create a workforce of self leaders ready to sail the course you set to successfully reach the destination. You'll pass the torch of power yet remain the guiding light. Your navigators will keep watch on the shoals and warn you of any dangers as you continually link to the organization's mission, vision, values, and strategies. You'll help keep individual job duties alive to benefit the entire organization.

12. Celebrate Success

Hosting parties to celebrate milestones is fun, but how else can you and your stakeholders enjoy success in a way that benefits your business?

One key to building on success is being able to repeat it. Do you know what instrumental factors you called upon again and again? What changes—temporary or permanent—occurred to achieve the goal? What new or improved processes you can use elsewhere in the company? What company strengths or values played important roles? What new ones were discovered? What other possibilities do they open for your company?

In your celebrations, I suggest you share the humility of great leaders and disperse the credit for success. Truly acknowledge those who contributed by recognizing—

- the essence of themselves they pulled from their core to support the effort.
- the magnitude of the efforts they undertook.
- the obstacles they overcame.

All this keeps the sparks alive for the huge ongoing effort required for sustainability.

What if you didn't reach your goal? Your greatest successes can come from learning from your mistakes. If you subscribe to this idea, then there is no failure. If there is no failure, then there can be no fear of failure, thus dissolving the biggest resistance to change. Acknowledge and celebrate this learning.

Chapter 6 discussed contriving intentional mistakes to exercise the change muscles. Certainly that would be futile without the mindset of believing in the value of the lessons learned. So harness the energy created and direct it to new goals and projects. Talk openly about the transferable characteristics, lessons, and skills to keep the excitement alive through the transition to new ventures.

Your greatest successes can come from learning from your mistakes. If you subscribe to this idea, then there is no failure. If there is no failure, then there can be no fear *of failure, thus dissolving the biggest resistance to change.*

THE SYSTAINERSHIP FUNCTION OF EMPOWERING PEOPLE

In this function of Systainership, leaders bring together internal and external stakeholders and partners throughout the organization. They're guided by the organization's mission, vision, and values to create more empowered, energized, and motivated participants in the business. This leadership function aligns corporate and personal fulfillment using a strengths-based, sustainable business model. Empowerment and energy is then dispersed throughout the organization through these people. Everyone reaps the rewards of a more sustainable business. See Figure 8.

SUSTAINABILITY BENEFITS THROUGH EMPOWERING PEOPLE

Your alignment with your company's vision, values, passion, and strengths not only serves in your leadership but in your company's performance as well. It's the foundation on which you stand when choosing what to work on, how to do it, what to delegate, and how to prioritize. It turns have-to's into want-to's as your actions emanate from positive energy instead of fear. It also provides a structure for having the right person in the right job. Without this congruity, you'll never achieve excellence or operate at your full potential.

Empowered employees are engaged in their work. They find fulfillment and meaning in what they do. They use their core strengths and talents in ways that align with their personal values and mission. They perform with intention, dedication, and loyalty, working with greater confidence to achieve extraordinary results.

Together, this creates employee satisfaction, motivation, increased productivity, a stable work force, and dedication to the financial and sustainability goals of your organization. Their increased resourcefulness paves the path to added contribution. They use more of their potential as they work together to foster synergy and harmony. Indeed, empowered employees become your organization's own advocacy group through the sheer enjoyment they receive from their jobs.

Declaring intentions creates strong feelings of rejuvenation, especially for commitments connected to a big and bold mission. Making a habit of such declarations leads to success in the effort. Why? Because when you put your intentions out in the world, synchronicity steps in and new

Systainership™

1.3 Empower People

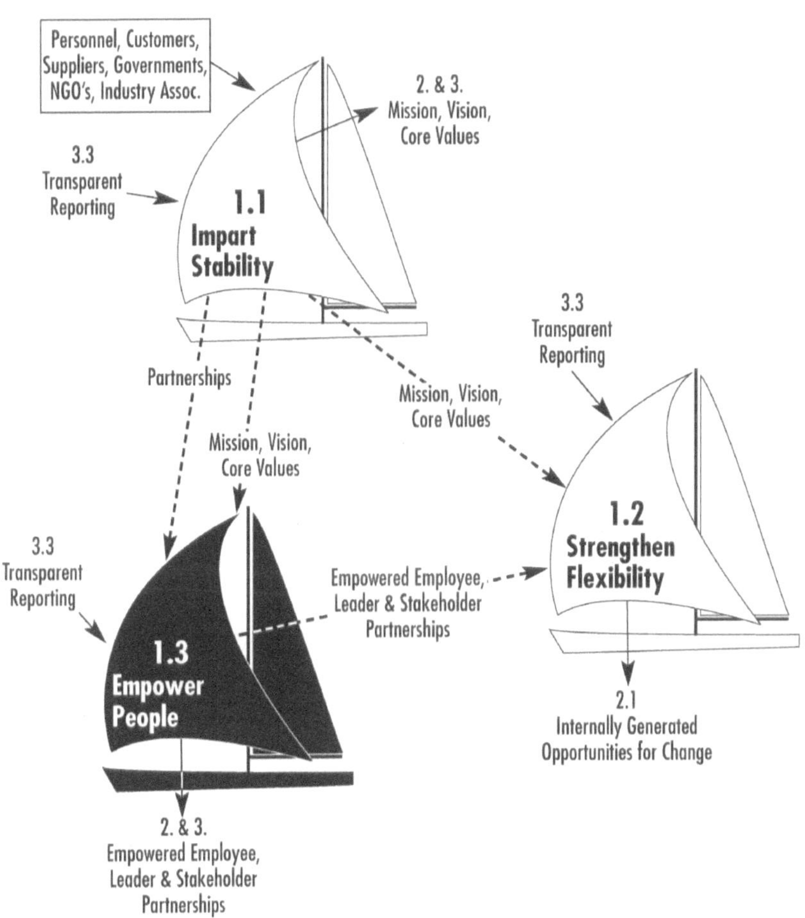

Figure 8

opportunities arise. A whole new energy gets cultivated; everyone feels vital and optimistic.

Overall, empowering yourself, your employees, and other stakeholders furthers the goals of your organization and creates sustainable growth.

APPLYING SYSTAINERSHIP

Coaching Questions to Move Your Organization Toward Empowering People

1. In the practice of inclusivity, can you name key executive leaders, sustainability champions, and change management artists who could be enrolled into your SEC team?
2. What area(s) of your organization would most benefit from an injection of fresh energy and motivation?
3. What is one core business strength that you believe is not being used to its potential?

For more coaching questions to help your business become more empowered and energized, go to www.SustainableBusinessSystems.com/bq.

Call to Action

Have your executive team identify one high-potential leadership candidate and co-create his/her job redefinition using empowerment practices noted in this chapter.

Your Insights on Empowering People

____

____

____

____

____

____

Moving Forward with the Systainership Function of Empowering People

What are five steps you can take now to lead your organization toward empowering people? Please list them in order of priority.

1. ______________________________________
2. ______________________________________
3. ______________________________________
4. ______________________________________
5. ______________________________________

PART THREE

Setting a Sustainable Course for the Longevity of Your Business

One ship sails east,
and another west,
by the self-same winds that blow.
'Tis the set of the sails,
and not the gales,
that tells the way we go.

~ ELLA WHEELER WILCOX (1850-1919)

CHAPTER

8

TOWARD A SUSTAINABLE ENTERPRISE

Greatness is not in where we stand, but in
what direction we are moving.
We must sail sometimes with the wind
and sometimes against it—but sail,
we must and not drift, nor lie at anchor.

~ OLIVER WENDELL HOLMES (1809-1894)

Setting a "Game-changing" Course—A Lesson from AISO.net

Millions of people from three years old to 103 are using the internet for business, personal, or entertainment reasons. The cumulative energy consumed to drive the worldwide web boggles the mind.

One company stands out as the first 100% *solar-powered* web hosting company. When AISO.net was founded in 1997, its leaders were determined to make that possible with their mission to become the "most reliable and responsible green web hosting company."[60] Within 13 years, it's become a truly green company. AISO.net doesn't need to rely on carbon offsets, planting trees, or other means to compensate for its carbon footprint; it simply doesn't have a carbon footprint at all!

Phil Nail, the company's co-owner and CTO (Chief Technical Officer), started AISO.net to form a highly energy-efficient data center while using available technology and solar power for some of its energy. Aiming to minimize pollution and preserve the earth's natural resources, he kept researching until he figured out how to power it 100% with solar energy. To power the data center, his technicians created the company's own electric grid using 120 solar panels and banks of batteries. It became operational 24/7 in 2002.[61]

Since 2002, the company has undertaken a number of other projects to reduce energy requirements and increase efficiencies using new technologies. Today, the resulting "Total Eco Web Servers" and company office in the Palm Desert Valley of California generate their own power needs from the sun, air, and water.[62]

A major milestone occurred in 2006 when the company switched from dedicated physical servers to virtual machines using the latest advances in data storage, efficient servers, and virtualization software. This led to an average increased processor usage of 10 to 75%.[63] In the same reconfiguration, it increased system redundancy. All these changes improved performance, security, and system reliability while keeping the mission whole. And others noticed. This move solidified the company's position on *Inc. Magazine*'s first list of Top 50 Green Companies in 2006.[64]

On its course to sustainability, AISO.net became the first public data center to join the U.S. Green Building Council—an organization that provides best building practices and certifies green buildings through its LEED certification program. As of 2010, AISO's next step is to conform to the required standards and apply for LEED certification.[65] Toward that end, it has already implemented an impressive list of green building design features into its new data center with innovative uses of available sun, air, water and new technologies. These changes have increased the company's eco-efficiencies as well.

Without doubt, AISO.net has raised the bar for data centers and created a new game in the industry. In fact, it was labeled a "game-changer" by the Environmental Defense Fund in its first

"Innovations Review 2008: Making Green the New Business as Usual." As stated in this review, the company's practices are clearly having long-term impact on this traditionally high-energy consumption industry. That includes having best sustainability practices integrated within every function of the organization, making it a truly innovative departure from business as usual.[66]

What about its bottom line? AISO.net has been profitable and debt-free since 1997 while averaging 20% annual growth. This is part of its transparent reporting as demonstrated on its website, www.aiso.net. Its success provides inspiration for other aspiring "green" companies.

DETERMINE THE DIRECTION FOR YOUR COMPANY

Having the support of a sustainable foundation under your company can aid you to set its direction and determine how you'll know if you're moving toward success. After all, how can you lead well if you don't know which way you want your company to head and how far you want to take it?

In today's world characterized by economic instability, political unrest, social challenges, and an endangered environment, the sustainability of businesses *and* the world are interdependent. Your company's direction, then, must create benefits that go well beyond the company itself. It determines what must change based on setting priorities and goals, establishing plans and budgets, allocating resources, and making a myriad of decisions. While mission, vision, and values address the "what" of an organization, setting direction tells everyone involved "how" to realize it within a sustainable business model, thus transforming challenges into strategies for success.

Your company's direction, then must create benefits that go well beyond the company itself.

Yet *setting* organizational direction is only half the task. *Communicating* it to employees, customers, and other stakeholders is equally important. You can't simplify your company's direction into one command to change its heading, rather it must be clearly understood and assimilated by everyone involved.

Communicating by storytelling has proven to be one effective way to convey messages meant to be remembered. Ancient tribes passed their history from generation to generation through storytelling. Saying what your company is destined to do and how it will make a difference enables you to convey your company's direction to others. Jeff Immelt, CEO of General Electric (GE), frequently takes his organization's story on the road. He speaks to business associations, university groups, and many others to spread the news of where GE is headed.

Why is telling your company's story effective? Because it helps people understand the importance of their contributions. Talking freely about problems and proposed solutions lead to realizing your overall goals and coming together to achieve those goals. Good storytelling can make a big difference for all!

STAY THE COURSE OR CHANGE IT

The extent of achievable sustainability depends on how fully it gets integrated into the core of a business. This includes the full scope of sustainability (described in Chapter 2) and the level to which your company aspires (described in Chapter 3). How do you lead your company to triple-based profitability? By making all efforts to achieve it the driving force of your company.

One way to do that is to set top-level goals that address global human challenges. A second way is to create a new "game" in your industry about how to conduct business. Interface is a large corporation that has adopted this game-changing approach; small companies like Hamakua Springs Country Farm, AISO.net, ShoreBank Pacific, and Pacific Biodiesel are also making sustainability their driving force. (You've met some of these companies already and will read about the others in the chapters that follow.)

A third way to lead your company sustainably is to integrate sustainable operations into your existing business. A fourth way is to introduce more sustainable products and services into your existing product line. (You'll see that most of the sustainability examples in this book combine these two strategies. Walmart started out using this third strategy but has shifted to follow in the footsteps of Interface under its consult.) The third and fourth strategies can be a means to becoming more sustainable while still determining what a comprehensive, sustainability-driven model for your business could look like.

For leaders wanting to create sustainability, it takes courage to ask questions like these:

- Can our products become sustainable?
- How can we profitably create a closed-loop system in our company?
- Can we unbundle the complexities of sustainability by examining local models?
- Are the costs of becoming a mission-driven organization affordable?

It takes even more courage to answer them because, like Interface's founder Ray Anderson, you may discover you need a rather large course correction in your business if you want to be sustainable for the long run. But asking and answering these questions is imperative in determining your business's core sustainability direction.

LEADER'S ROLE IN CREATING DIRECTION

In this fast-paced world, every company is inundated with challenges and opportunities. You may find it daunting to choose among the myriad of paths to manifest its vision. It requires a blend of art and science to determine how your company will achieve it. Indeed, it can be tough just to figure out the first step!

As a leader, it's your responsibility to guide people in your organization to know where to focus their energy and resources. After all, not all opportunities are viable; priorities must be set. However, limiting your choices too soon can be problematic. It's important to examine opportunities with an open mind first—the approach AISO.net has taken over its 14-year growth. I suggest being adventurous when looking at your options. Analyze "status quo" areas of the business to determine if they still fit where the company is headed. Select certain areas of exploration suited to your business and let loose with innovation, brainstorming, research, and creativity.

Using visioning techniques can help to develop potential scenarios that would provide sustainable ways to move forward in each area. Look for the true genius of your company to blossom here. Yes, it takes discipline to refrain from spouting off limitations before the visioning is complete. Preface your discussions of new concepts with this question: "What might this look like in a sustainable world?."

Preface your discussions of new concepts with this question: "What might this look like in a sustainable world?"

Once you have conceived lots of "crazy" strategic ideas, reel them back in by acknowledging the realities of the business. You'll find that the strong strategies will align better with more aspects—vision, resources, technology, sustainability, profitability—than the weak ones. You'll identify strategic dependencies and reorganize the strategies for better leverage. At this stage, you would make a complete business case for the sustainable strategies as you assess and prioritize them. These would become part of the alignment analysis presented in Chapter 11, which includes the application of sustainability models called TNS (The Natural Step), Cradle-to-Cradle, or Zero Footprint.

Once you're moving forward, how do you assess the level of success achieved? Through the critical success factors introduced in Chapter 12. You would lead the selection of the most vital factors that impact achieving the vision, the goals, and the individual strategies. Ideally, all subordinate measures, including those that assess business unit and employee performance, roll into the critical success factors that link to the overarching vision of the company. This will strengthen the unity

Systainership™
2. Set a Sustainable Course
3.3 Transparent Reporting
1.1 Mission, Vision, Core Values
1.3 Empowered Employee, Leader & Stakeholder Partnerships
External Opportunities and Challenges
1.2 Internally Generated Opportunities for Change
2.1 Create Focus
Focus Statements
1.3 Empowered Employee, Leader & Stakeholder Partnerships
1.1 Mission, Vision, Core Values
3.3 Transparent Reporting
2.2 Invent Strategic Scenarios
Strategy Scenarios
3.1 Critical Success Factors
1.3 Empowered Employee, Leader & Stakeholder Partnerships
1.1 Mission, Vision, Core Values
3.3 Transparent Reporting
2.4 Establish Critical Success Factors
Aligned Sustainable Strategy
1.3 Empowered Employee, Leader & Stakeholder Partnerships
1.1 Mission, Vision, Core Values
3.3 Transparent Reporting
2.3 Assess Sustainability Alignment
3.1 Aligned Sustainable Strategy

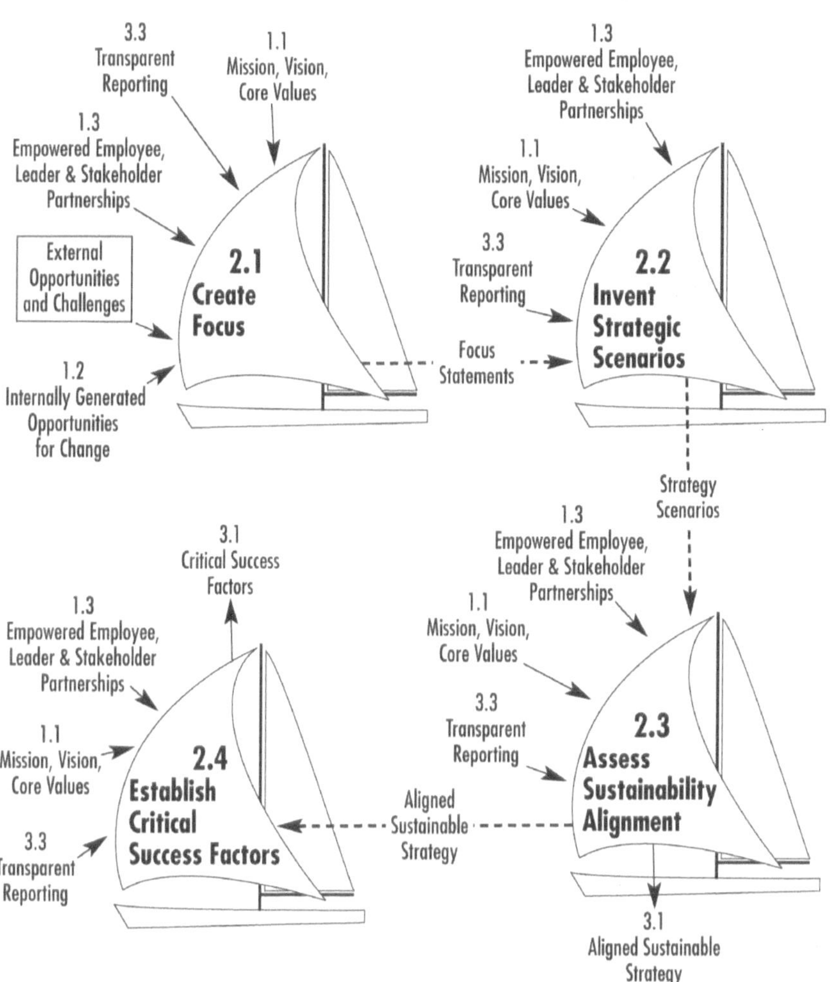

Figure 9

of the strategies—as well as the fortitude of the participants—by connecting the work to a meaningful effort.

Notice this: The leadership function of setting a sustainable course alternates between *expanding the ideas* and *cinching them in* before a smooth course can be selected. Figure 9 shows the relationship among these functions. They are developed in detail in the next four chapters with discussions on how to—

- create focus.
- invent strategic scenarios.
- assess sustainability alignment.
- establish critical success factors.

Chapters 9, 10, 11, and 12 discuss how to integrate sustainability into each of these key leadership functions.

CHAPTER

9

MAINTAIN STEADY FOCUS AT THE HELM

It comes from saying no to 1,000 things to make sure we don't get on the wrong track or try to do too much.

~ STEVE JOBS (1955-2011), BUSINESS WEEK ONLINE, OCT. 12, 2004

World's Largest Retailer Zeros In—A Lesson from Walmart

Some people gasp when you use the name "Walmart" and the word "sustainability" in the same sentence. But no one can deny the progress Walmart has made since October 2005 when then CEO H. Lee Scott announced Walmart's plan to step up its sustainability initiatives. Its leaders have set out to transform the company so it runs on 100% renewable energy and produces zero waste.[67]

How overwhelmed would you feel making plans like that for *your* company? I believe the secret to such progress is focus. Walmart's focus and progress are evident in its on-going sustainability reports posted on its website for all to see.[68]

Walmart's 2009 report, developed under the Global Reporting Initiative (GRI) guidelines, demonstrates the focus its leaders have chosen.[69] The economic section of this report reveals the massive retailer's focus on these five key financial indicators:

1. Net sales
2. Net sales increase
3. Operating income
4. Earnings per share
5. Dividends per share

Many more financial measurements could be monitored and managed, but in the interest of creating focus, Walmart's leaders have chosen to concentrate on this set. In the environmental section, they have outlined these three key goals:

1. To be supplied 100% by renewable energy
2. To create zero waste
3. To sell products that sustain our resources and the environment[70]

In the social arena, they have selected these three areas of concentration:

1. Responsible sourcing including ethical purchasing and supply chain
2. Associate opportunities
3. Charitable giving[71]

Due to the size of the organization, the number and size of projects in each of the three arenas are more extensive than any small-to-medium-sized company could undertake. But that doesn't undermine Walmart's lesson in focus—something that could be scaled to your organization.

EVER TRIED TO JUGGLE ORANGES?

At best, most people can keep only two or three oranges in the air at once. In business, this translates to juggling bottom lines and their related projects. Twentieth-century business leaders got used to dealing with the traditional *financial* bottom lines, having perhaps 10 to 12 measures yet focusing on a fewer number while keeping the others in their peripheral view.

In the latter decades of the 20th century, EPA, OSHA, and other government agencies imposed new regulations, operational limits, and reporting requirements on the environmental and operating performance of businesses. That happened before companies took the initiative to consider which environmental and social bottom lines would be best for their business model. As you may have experienced, agency compliance can distract your business from what's important to its sustainability *beyond* compliance. Today, determining *additional* environmental and social bottom lines to further the sustainability of both the organization and the world can be downright overwhelming. But not keeping a sharp focus can create operational nightmares.

Behavioral scientists say that the human mind can't juggle more than three to five things at a time. This also applies to organizations. In my coaching engagements, I often encounter clients trying to do too many things at once without having a clear focus on what or why. Scattering resources around is never as beneficial as sharply focusing them. What's the trick? To determine the capacity and priorities for your organization in an ever more complex scenario.

Behavioral scientists say that the human mind can't juggle more than three to five things at a time. This also applies to organizations

EXAMPLE OF CREATING FOCUS

The carpet manufacturer Interface, Inc. you learned about in Chapter 5 (with more of their journey to come in Chapter 11) is considered the industry leader in sustainability. Ray Anderson, its founder and past chairman, talked of his company's path to sustainability as "climbing one face of Mount Sustainability after another." He wisely never intended to try to climb them all at once, even though he could see them all ahead of the summit.[72]

As part of its mission, Interface created its own consulting firm, InterfaceRAISE™, to share success with other large companies following in its path. In fact, this consulting was instrumental in helping Walmart identify its own mountains and creating areas of business focus on its sustainability journey.

In sustainability leadership, having a strong focus takes leaders from feeling overwhelmed to moving forward, from confusion to clarity, and from reaction to proactivity. Executing the function is guided by a company's strong vision and mission in today's fast-paced world. Businesses can't wait five or ten years for their next strategic plans to be developed and published. Routinely creating and maintaining focus is essential for the survival of any company in today's business environment.

Businesses can't wait five or ten years for their next strategic plans to be developed and published.

In optical terms, focus is where light rays converge (come together). In business, focus is where resources converge. Bringing together resources leverages their effectiveness but when they get too scattered, their effectiveness diminishes.

As an example of this, look at how you spend your time. On days when you focus or concentrate on specific tasks, your productivity and effectiveness soar. When your attention is pulled in different directions, your effectiveness suffers because you don't give any one task the level of attention it needs. Creating blocks of time to focus on specifics allows those areas of your business to produce a stronger impact.

7 STEPS TO CREATE FOCUS FOR YOUR BUSINESS

Evaluating the opportunities and challenges you face with the goal of creating a powerful focus includes the 7 steps that follow.

Step 1: Describe the opportunities and challenges you're company is considering.

Opportunities and challenges continually bombard your organization from all directions, with some being internally generated (as you saw in the function of creating flexibility in Chapter 6). How you handle these affects the sustainability of your business, even those directly related to sustainability. The first step is to list each opportunity and challenge along with descriptions that state the source and potential impact for the company.

Step 2: Decompose each opportunity and challenge.

Decomposition means breaking apart an opportunity or challenge into its fundamental components. You'd look at all the factors, issues, intentions, fears, and key players separately while identifying the boundaries of each issue. Then you can identify smaller critical areas requiring specific attention.

No doubt looking at the whole can be a daunting task. That's why whenever any of my clients feel overwhelmed, we disentangle the situation into its smaller, separate issues. Often, the majority of these aren't the source of the overwhelm and can be dismissed, which makes the size and scope of the actual offending issues seem more manageable.

The Green CEO itself provides an excellent example of decomposition. Faced with the challenge of pressure from consumers, stockholders, and other interested parties, many leaders want to make their companies greener and more sustainable, yet how to tackle the overall concept seems overwhelming. Hence, information in this book helps them proactively select and break down the "green" and "sustainable" leadership concepts into manageable areas of focus.

Step 3: Analyze each opportunity and challenge listed.

Addressing elemental components of your business, analysts typically present you with the impact of each—the pros and cons, the who, what, when, where, how and why—in the context of key issues facing the company and the industry. This includes conveying the history of each issue while assessing related strengths and weaknesses within the company, industry, technology, market, competition, stakeholders, and so on. They'd include an analysis of the findings and how they apply to the company's mission, goals, sustainability and strategy. They'd also address the effect of each issue on the organization's structure, personnel, and processes, and they'd offer recommendations.

Your job as a leader is clear: to guide your analysts on how to create clarity around each issue.

For any company and especially small ones, this analysis needs to be tailored to the resources available. Because leaders of small organizations are intimately involved in all areas of their companies, a more casual approach to the analysis than large organizations would take is appropriate. This is coupled by using your informed intuition to indicate where analysis resources should be focused.

Cross-disciplinary teams, addressed in Chapter 6, are equally important when setting the make-up of your analytical team. Remember to include differing perspectives that will render increased value to the company.

Step 4: Dig out root causes.

The superficial appearance of opportunities and challenges can be misleading because biased solutions may be imbedded within them. This means instead of expressing the actual challenge, one might unconsciously climb up the inference ladder and present a solution that seems viable, yet is itself still a challenge or issue. Here's an example.

While consulting with the County of Hawaii to create a community development plan, I was able to oversee the input collected from county residents. In one particular area, people had to commute more than 100 miles a day for employment. When asked what they wanted in their community over the next 20 years, many said they'd like to see resorts, prisons, big-box stores, and other large business enterprises. But what was at the root cause of these suggestions? A need to have more local jobs. These large-scale suggestions were the only "solutions" they could come up with to address the inherent problem of minimal local employment opportunities. This misleading approach could result in creating something totally out of culture for this island community.

Digging down early in the process to harvest these root issues saves time and resources when evaluating the opportunities and challenges of your business. How can you delve beneath the symptoms? One of the best ways is to ask: "Well, if you had that (solution, implementation, feature, etc.), what would it give you? And if you had that, what would the benefit be?" Another approach is to apply the incessant questioning of "why" as small children do. Taiichi Ohno, of Toyota, formalized this into the "5 Why" method of rooting out causes. Although there's nothing magical about the number 5, the point is to keep asking "why" until you get beyond the symptoms and arrive at a related problem within a business function or process that can be corrected.

Step 5: Categorize common elements.

This calls for looking at the root issues across the identified opportunities and challenges to find commonalities, then categorize how they relate to each other. The resulting relationships could be defined by location, business function, effect on a particular triple-based bottom line, product line, market, timeframe, environmental or social impact, or any other slice of business. Categorizing also helps clarify the related business impact needed for the next step—prioritizing.

Step 6: Prioritize the opportunities and challenges.

Strategic prioritizing requires looking at where the largest business impacts can be made to advance your sustainable business model and the relative costs and resources for achieving them. During this high-level analysis, you may also consider the effects of technical maturity on the organization, learning curve requirements, labor intensity, ability to identify clear-cut steps, and so on. Taking a holistic view of these factors at this stage helps you—

- resolve obvious strategic conflicts of resource allocation.
- plan for tiered strategies that support a phased implementation of your sustainable business model.
- keep costs low.
- leverage partnership and stakeholder relationships.
- control the impact of proposed changes on product and service delivery.

Once you've prioritized the opportunities and challenges, you'd create areas of focus for your business. You'd then transform all focuses selected into strategic scenarios. These in turn would be thoroughly screened through a sustainability lens and undergo a complete business alignment further along in Systainership.

Step 7: Create strategic tiers.

The list of root opportunities and challenges you're prioritizing might surpass your company's ability to execute. Lee Scott's corporate directive of 2005 was more than Walmart could undertake at once. Like Mr. Scott, you, too, need to select the focus of your business. Using the priorities list prepared by your analytical team—along with your corporate mission, vision, and sustainability goals—you can artfully determine your company's capacity at this time. Take Steve Jobs's advice from this chapter's beginning quotation and just say "no" to many attractive paths you could take. You want to stay on track and avoid overextending your resources. The strategic tiers you identify will sustainably bridge the gap from where your business is now to where you want it to be. (I define strategic tiers as phases of a partitioned yet cohesive strategy.)

The strategic tiers you identify will sustainably bridge the gap from where your business is now *to* where you want it to be.

After you've been through this once, your baseline provides direction for assessing new opportunities and challenges against it periodically. When do you do that? Adam Werbach, in *Strategy for Sustainability*, says that the timeframe for strategic decisions has become so short that analyzing new strategic direction needs to be done daily. Clearly, that would be too time-consuming for owners of small-to-medium-sized businesses. It also requires confidence in your organization's stability and willingness to change everything else. However, realize that the old 5-to-10-year strategic planning efforts have become obsolete. And your business could become obsolete too if you don't tailor the timing for reviewing your business's focus to the needs and the pace of the change it's facing.

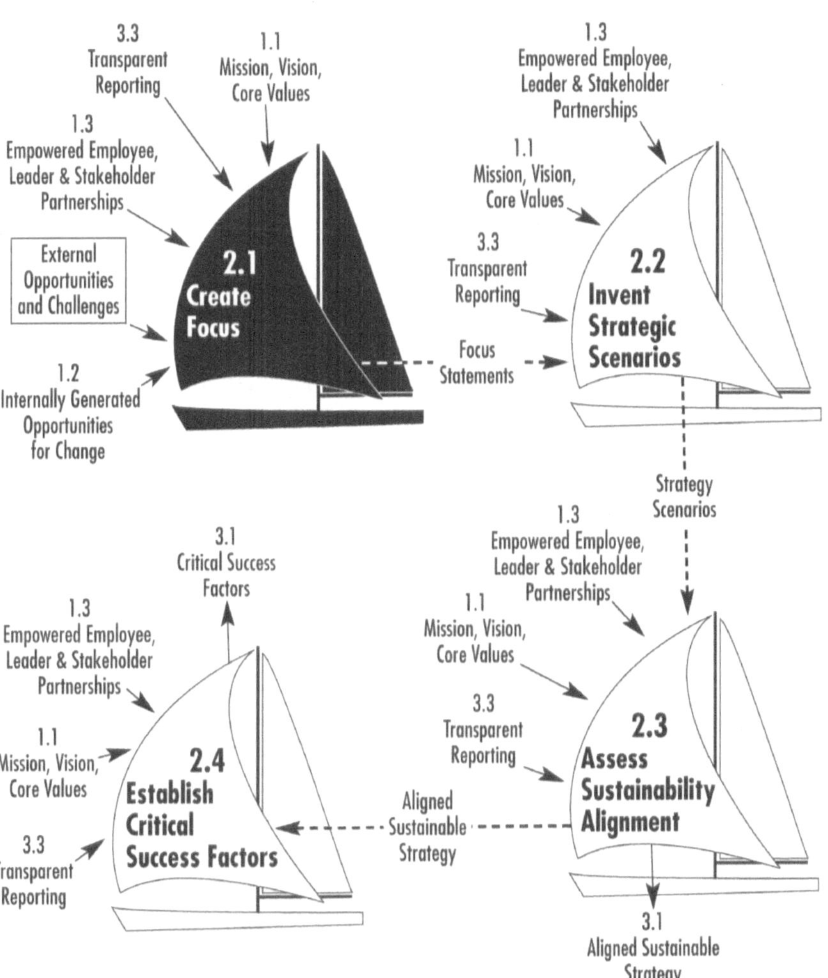

Figure 10

THE SYSTAINERSHIP FUNCTION OF CREATING FOCUS

Within Systainership, creating focus is essential in leading your business on a sustainable course. It's not a linear step but an embedded, iterative function within your leadership toolkit. You empower the best analytical minds of your organization. Together, you look at all the opportunities and challenges bombarding your organization from all directions, including those of your own making. Your team assists you by clarifying all the issues and getting them into a comparable format so they can be assessed and prioritized for selecting your company's direction. Then you can express that direction in clear, concise statements communicated to your organization's visionaries who will undertake the next step. See Figure 10.

Leading the analytical process (as described in this chapter) differs from how you lead the visionary process (in the next chapter) because the mindset and skill sets of the two teams differ, requiring different leadership approaches. Word of caution: Don't jump the gun and lead your group into brainstorming solutions before reducing the issues to their *root* causes and assessing their full business impact.

SUSTAINABILITY BENEFITS THROUGH CREATING FOCUS

The real power in focus comes from your ability to take responsibility—for your company, your community, the environment, your stockholders, and ultimately your company's contribution to the world. Focus fosters an acceptance of things as they are at this moment, even though you wished they were different. You're able to expedite forward movement with a concentrated effort in the areas chosen. These areas become the center of activity where resources get allocated most effectively and you're able to respond more creatively to current problems.

Creating focus shifts your mindset from overwhelm to confidence so you're ready to generate sustainable, powerful, and transformational business results.

Creating focus shifts your mindset from overwhelm to confidence so you're ready to generate sustainable, powerful, and transformational business results. It also gives you greater confidence in making decisions that will support both the short-term and long-term needs of your business as you overcome obstacles and pursue the most beneficial opportunities for your organization.

APPLYING SYSTAINERSHIP

Coaching Questions to Move Your Organization Toward Creating Focus

1. What is the biggest challenge your company is facing today?
2. For the challenge you cited, who are the key analysts throughout your organization with the skills to break it down into its fundamental elements?
3. What would it take to assemble those analysts into an issue focus team to accomplish that?

For more coaching questions to help your business create greater focus, go to www.SustainableBusinessSystems.com/bq.

Call to Action

Set up a focus team to analyze your company's biggest challenge you just identified. Have the members break it down into its base elements so each can be included in a focus analysis.

Your Insights on Creating Focus

____

____

____

____

____

____

Moving Forward with the Systainership Function of Creating Focus

What are five steps you can take now to lead your organization toward creating focus? Please list them in order of priority.

1. ____
2. ____
3. ____
4. ____
5. ____

CHAPTER

10

ENVISION THE HORIZON

Here's to the crazy ones, the misfits, the rebels, the troublemakers, the round pegs in the square holes… the ones who see things differently—they're not fond of rules… You can quote them, disagree with them, glorify or vilify them, but the only thing you can't do is ignore them because they change things… they push the human race forward, and while some may see them as the crazy ones, we see genius, because the ones who are crazy enough to think that they can change the world, are the ones who do.

~ STEVE JOBS (1955-2011)

One Visionary Mind Leads to an Inventive International Conglomerate—A Lesson from Walt Disney

This company touches me because of how it entertained me as a child and has since grown into a household name worldwide—The Walt Disney Company.

Today, Disney stands tall as a corporate leader in both sustainability and innovation—all stemming from the creative mind of one man, Walt Disney. When he founded his company in the 1920s, Walt felt an awesome responsibility to influence the future worldwide. And it's become a dream come true; in 2009, the company found itself on *Business Week*'s Most

Innovative Corporations List, Forbes.com's 100 Corporations That Will Survive 100 Years, and Global 100's Most Sustainable Corporations in the World List. What a legacy this company has built since it first brought fantasy characters to life in hand-drawn cartoons.

Creativity and innovation have been the company's duel driving forces since 1923 when Walt set up a small cartoon studio. He had an uncanny talent for envisioning cartoon characters in action. He humanized them with facial expressions and animated them through sequences of images made into storyboards, later delivered to the public through the advent of his television program "The Wonderful World of Disney." That was just the start. Walt said, "Curiosity keeps leading us down new paths. We're always exploring and experimenting."

Although Walt died in 1966, his company has continued to thrive. It has grown to five business segments: media networks, parks and resorts, studio entertainment, consumer products, and interactive media.[73] Its founding principles of imagination and innovation remain key to all aspects of the business. Roy Disney, Walt's nephew, recognized how critical they are to the dynasty's success. In 1987, he established the Disney Legends program to recognize individual employees for their imaginative innovations. Awards are given in disciplines from administration and animation to "imagineering" and economic research.[74] As an example, Disney legend Card Walker who became president in 1971, evolved this family-owned company into a major global corporation under his administration. Today's list of legends includes more than 225 innovative contributors, not counting Walt himself.[75]

The innovations keep coming. In early 2010, Disney and its Disney Interactive Studios developed new applications compatible with iPhones and iPod Touch devices. For example, the Muppets Animal Drummer game puts users into the drummer's seat electronically. You can "let your inner animal come out and play" as you match Animal's notes and timing. You score points based on your accuracy, and the game gets more challenging as you improve. It's just one way Disney characters are being brought to mobile audiences.

The company has also stepped up its promotional activities through product bundling and customer relationship-building using Disney Interactive Studios and Disney Consumer Products. Before the movie *The Princess and the Frog* was ever released, for example, young girls could buy a package and host slumber parties complete with interactive video games, dolls, costumes, bedding, decorations, party supplies—all movie-related. They could even download a party tip sheet at the movie's website.[76]

In the arena of sustainability, Disney has divided its focus into five areas: children and family, content and products, environment, community, and workplace.[77] In the interest of transparency, it published an extensive 2008 sustainability report at corporate.disney.go.com/responsibility/index.html. If you read the report, you'll see that company sustainability metrics are absent. However, its narrative highlights outstanding achievements like these:

- 1960 – The company set aside nearly one-third of Walt Disney World property in Florida as a wildlife conservation area in perpetuity.
- 1993 – The company purchased 8500 acres of at-risk Everglades headwaters and formed the Nature Conservancy's Disney Wilderness Preserve.
- All Disney resorts in Florida have achieved the Florida Green Lodging Certification.
- Total corporate donations for 2008 totaled $209 million in a combination of cash, in-kind donations, and product donations.
- Employee volunteers donated nearly 500,000 hours and raised $1.7 million through their participation in community projects.
- The Disney workplace continues to foster a safe, inclusive, respectful environment.

The company's content and products are developed with high ethical standards to give families a feeling of security when bringing Disney into their homes.

---

12 TOOLS TO ENCOURAGE VISION AND INNOVATION

Vision goes beyond the realm of what is and into the realm of what could be, making it the seed of sustainable change. Combined with opportunity, vision helps your company realize new paths to success. Not all companies possess the innovative prowess of Disney, but any company can improve its innovative skills by creating its own "imagineering" toolbox, which include the tools described in this chapter.

Vision goes beyond the realm of what is *and into the realm of* what could be, *making it the seed of sustainable change.*

In *Good to Great*, Jim Collins shows that companies with "personal best" lasting power practice what he terms the Hedgehog Concept that asks these questions:

- What you are deeply passionate about?
- What can you be the best in the world at?
- What best drives your economic engine?[78]

To create sustainable strategies in the context of the Hedgehog questions, I present 12 visioning tools that will take your organization well beyond its vision statement. If your company is re-examining its vision statement with fresh eyes, you will also find these tools extremely helpful.

1. *Foster Curiosity*

   Early on, I learned that necessity and curiosity are the mothers of invention. My father instilled in me the belief that I could have anything I wanted if I put my mind to it—something atypical for young girls in the 1960s. The questions I learned to ask started with "How can I" rather than "Why can't I …"

Necessity can be a strong motivator. The U.S. government's space program that sent a man to the moon in 1969 in its race against the Soviet Union sparked the creation of new technologies, products, and materials that have found their way into mainstream living. Today, industries are creatively addressing environmental stewardship issues. Continued needs like this will motivate people to develop innovative solutions.

You don't need to be stymied by the challenges you face in business. Instead, open your mind to curiosity. Translate each need into "how, what, who, where, when, and why" questions. Drill down until you can't think of any more questions, then start asking "what if …"

2. *Be Open to Possibility*

This means letting go of the notion that there's a scarce, finite number of solutions to the problems that fit into the box you've drawn around your organization. It means being comfortable with living "in the questions," giving them room to breathe and time to incubate. It means embracing an uncertain future while knowing that innovative solutions capable of transporting your company into the future will percolate. Answers will more likely surface in large numbers when you engage others in your passion.

Being open means differentiating between survival and survival thinking, between scarcity and scarcity thinking, between comparison and competition, between attachment and anxiety. It requires shifting your mindset from pessimism to possibility—from what is to what could be.

3. *Assemble "Hot" Mastermind Groups*

Are you thinking, "I don't see this kind of creativity pouring forth in my organization, so where will all these creative ideas come from?" In an organization that doesn't support creativity as part of its culture, innovative people remain hidden. They'll only surface when your culture becomes open and receptive to creativity.

In their book *The Art of Innovation*, Tom Kelly and Jonathan Littman recommend forming project teams[79]—teams that last for a project's lifespan, whether for a few days or an extended time. They advocate announcing creativity projects with passion and seeing who steps forward to be part of the effort. People who know themselves as "Creatives" will find ways to participate; just plant the seeds and watch them grow. That said, choose team members with diversity in mind. Align team members' passions, challenge their suggestions, and you'll discover extraordinary resources within your company.

Don't overlook the power of Web 2.0 technology and social networks to involve your customers in creating solutions. For example, *Inc. Magazine*'s special report exalts the company Threadless for its creative business model. This t-shirt manufacturer solicits all of its designs from its customers. By knowing what the customers want, Threadless leaders have never produced a product that didn't completely sell out.[80]

A similar approach is being applied to create open-source software. For example, Google is opening its Google Wave resource to the open-source software world, inviting users to help design and test its features.

How could you take this concept to promote innovation in your industry?

4. *Recognize Opportunity*

Sometimes you can't hear the rat-a-tat of opportunity knocking because you're preoccupied with the everyday struggle of running your business. Plus all ideas that come your way won't be appropriate to follow, so what do you do? Make choices based on your vision and mission. Seeing the right opportunity might be as simple as recognizing an insight in the right context. Or one might pop up during a top-down search. Recognizing opportunities leads to a preliminary vision that could then be formalized and elaborated on. You could also find the right opportunity by gathering information and then use creativity tools to generate insight, incubate ideas, and add value.

You might also discover insight through conducting business assessments. In *Greening Your Business*, Daniel Sitarz provides a basic framework for assessing environmental sustainability with useful worksheets, documented strategies, and valuable guides to best practices, which can be used as comparisons.[81] Similarly, an assessment of your business' community support and stewardship could be helpful. Small businesses can phase these in over time while setting priorities based on their needs and areas of focus.

5. *Transform Challenge*

Challenges constantly test an organization's resources and capabilities, putting a hurdle or obstacle on its current path to success. But when you use your curiosity to view challenges as opportunities and breakdowns as breakthroughs, you can get creative results.

Leaders who swiftly convert challenge to opportunity and negativity to optimism put themselves squarely at the helm of their businesses. These days, the accelerated growth of the human population—combined with the stress it puts on our environmental systems—challenges everyone. Yet it also presents opportunities to nurture triple-based businesses that contribute to environmental regeneration and community support. What a world it could be!

Of course, converting challenge to opportunity takes practice at all levels of the organization. In the weekly coaching journal I send to my clients, I include this question: "What is one challenge you will turn into an opportunity this week?" This question exercises their "conversion" muscles, turns negativity to positivity, and keeps their minds open for creating new opportunities. You can ask this question whenever employees get entrenched in negative thinking. It will help them transform challenges into opportunities in their own realm.

6. *Stimulate Creativity*

Some people are born with incredibly creative minds while others need help to stimulate their creativity. A wonderful resource is Thinkertoys by Michael Milchalko because it contains 29 linear and intuitive thinking exercises.[82] (As a nonlinear thinker, my two favorite techniques from this book are mind mapping and brainstorming.) Tap into the hidden creative talents of all your people by stimulating it every chance you get.

7. *Nurture Whole-Brain Thinking*

I don't believe it's accurate to separate people into right-brain and left-brain thinkers. After all, the right and left sides of the brain have to work as a cohesive unit. However, most people behaviorally favor attributes of one or the other.

Thus, business has been dominated for centuries by left-brain thinkers, a world of logic, sequence, language, analysis, and details. Artists—generally right-brained people—"see" things at once, sense spatial relationships, assimilate the elements of a situation in context, and synthesize the big picture of a situation. They entered the business world when marketing innovations added sensual appeal to benefit-laden product or service descriptions as a way to increase sales.

Historically, left-brain thinking has been more highly valued in American society and in its public school system, based on a 19th-century Prussian model designed to homogenize people and produce a manageable society.[83] Left-brain thinking was also highly valued in the Information Age and rewarded in driving businesses. In contrast, students who were predominately right-brained were neglected in schools, undervalued during the Information Age, and overlooked in business organizations.

With the nature of business changing, though, today's right-brained contingent now sets direction through artistry fed by the artists' empathetic outlooks, ability to vision long-range outcomes, and canniness to transcend black-and-white perceptions. A talented organization integrates the best of all minds, balancing right- and left-brain strengths, art and science, logic and imagination.

Where does artistry fit into your organization?

8. *Maintain Well-being*

The effort of leaders to maintain their well-being benefits from the resulting peak performance and full engagement of well-sustained individuals. Who thinks their best when they're tired?

And how can you generate new ideas when you're stressed out?

Taking responsibility for the well-being of your body, mind, and soul maintains the physical, mental, and emotional strength you need to generate creativity. The simple actions of exercise, good nutrition, meditation, and journaling keep you in top form. If you lead by example, you can transform your whole organization into fully engaged individuals who have a higher capacity for creativity and innovation.

9. *Envision Strategies*

Envisioning strategies for change requires applying creative thinking to current opportunities within the context of your business direction. A strong visioning process transforms opportunities in any area or at any level of your company into potential business strategies that can be sustainable.

Just like waving Disney's magic wand, you can assess what your company could achieve if it took advantage of a particular opportunity. Try "back casting," which is used by many companies and is part of The Natural Step process. The back casting technique starts by painting a picture of what the future will look like and then imagining, in reverse, the strategic steps it took to get there.

Imagine your sustainable strategy as the first step of the back casting process. This removes the ideation from current limiting beliefs and from the imposing restrictions forecasting creates in areas where current knowledge might be lacking. Use it to open your business to new possibilities.

10. *Build Sustainable Scenarios*

From the strategic ideas that the visionaries of your organization generate, sustainable scenarios are built. How? By prioritizing the challenges your company faces and synergizing opportunities to leverage your resources well. The result? Creating strategies that have the greatest value for your organization.

Your visionaries can also evaluate the contribution of each scenario to the sustainability of the business at each of the five levels (as presented in Chapter 3), including the sustainable vision you have for the company.

The last part of the scenario statement makes the connection with the "how" of the strategy and moves the ideas from the realm of *possibility* into the realm of *probability*. In this area, applying sustainability methodologies such as The Natural Step or Cradle-to-Cradle helps stimulate ideas. (You'll see how these methodologies can be applied in greater depth to assessing sustainability alignment in Chapter 11.)

Realize that any particular business challenge can be transformed into multiple opportunities and scenarios. These scenarios can be further grouped into design stages of growth within your company.

11. *Testing Knowledge Through Experience*
Next, you want to have the strategic scenarios screened by people outside your visionary team. Select industry experts or academic specialists who might even come from other organizations. You'll also benefit from your company's learning experiences gained from previous mistakes, adversities that have been overcome, and even anti-role modeling. If the scenarios "pass" these outsider reviews with flying colors, the probability of them working will increase.

12. *Be Willing to Hold the Creative Tension*
When envisioned strategies don't easily lend themselves to sustainable scenarios, frustration or anxiety could result. Realize that the greater the related challenges are to the organization, the more intense these feelings can be. This is called the creative tension between *where you are* and *where you want to be*, and it's fueled by not knowing how to get there.

To succeed, your organization must build tolerance for this tension. It must keep the vision alive and strong while the visionary team exercises its innovative practices and allows the synergy of intuitive creation to unfold. If this tension is held at a healthy level, then creative innovations will flow.

THE SYSTAINERSHIP FUNCTION OF INVENTING STRATEGIC SCENARIOS

In Systainership, this is the point at which you lead your organization to switch from the logical function of creating focus to a visionary one of inventing strategic scenarios, as noted in Figure 11. Use focus statements to invent innovative business solutions that support the arching business vision and contribute to its sustainability on one or more levels. Lead your teams to transform your focus statements into strategic scenarios using various creativity and innovation processes. The reward? It opens up new possibilities—and potentially new horizons—for your business.

However, don't expect this to be a 1:1 transformation of focus statement to strategic scenario. Rather, the pool of selected opportunities are looked at from holistic viewpoints and synergized to create the best approaches. At this point, these are still strategic scenarios needing to be assessed for business alignment. In the assessment, the viability and sustainability for the business are analyzed in depth before specific strategies are put in place, as discussed in Chapter 11.

SUSTAINABILITY BENEFITS THROUGH INVENTING STRATEGIC SCENARIOS

Developing potential strategies increases your commitment to achieve your company vision and, in doing so, increases its likelihood for success. Everyone involved senses the leaders' commitment. In turn, that boosts individual commitments and penetrates the organization as a whole. The scenarios themselves open up further creativity and thought, improving and strengthening the strategic options for your company to evaluate and pursue. This supports it in achieving both long-term and short-term triple-based

Everyone involved senses the leaders' commitment. In turn, that boosts individual commitments and penetrates the organization as a whole.

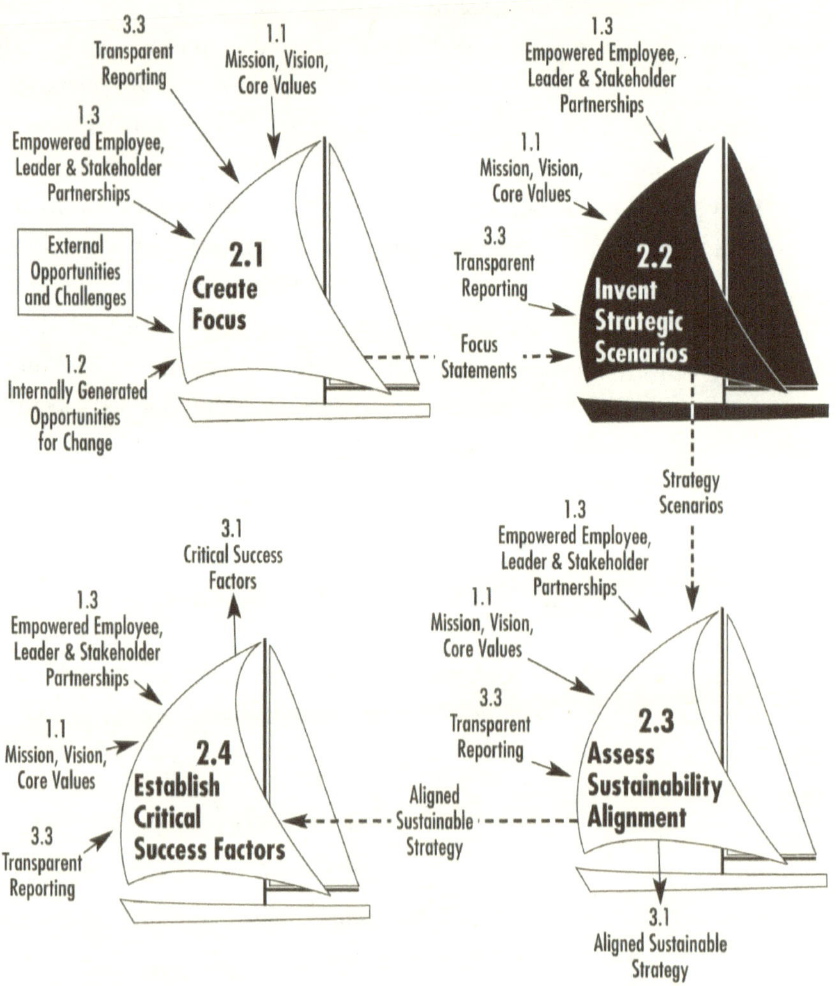

Figure 11

profitability. Shaping your strategic scenarios provides options for how to get there.

You can lead your organization to shape these strategic scenarios at all levels of your organization. From a corporate-level vision (discussed in Chapter 5) to individual employee-level visions, you can sense your company being pulled forward into the future. You'll find the strength of commitment, motivation, and engagement to be directly proportional to the strength and alignment of these collective visions and strategies. The greater detail and depth behind the vision, the greater the power it will have. That gives your legacy plan—the penultimate picture of where your organization is headed—greater thrust than ever.

The function of inventing these scenarios gets your organization out of the usual inside-the-box thinking to come up with creative and valuable solutions. These strategic scenarios (after assessing sustainability alignment presented in the next chapter) follow vision and focus in forming the next important guideline in decision-making.

They also—

- build deeper camaraderie and loyalty among all stakeholders, which encourages collaboration and synergy.
- nurture an open culture in which new ideas are welcome.
- boost confidence for all to move forward with greater efficiency and productivity.
- provide direction for a clear marketing message.

Indeed, shaping strategy moves the company toward greater sustainability in three ways. First, the scenarios directly support your vision of a sustainable organization. Second, the sustainability lens is incorporated into any strategy created (as discussed in Chapter 11). Third, they lead to more focused activities and better resource allocation, thus contributing to greater sustainability.

For leaders of small organizations, it's important not to confuse "doing" with "being" or "functionality" with "people." All companies need to maximize the use of their resources, including their staff. So creating awareness of these considerations among a few talented people within your organization can go a long way toward achieving this kind of inventiveness for developing sustainable solutions.

Indeed, once strong strategies have been put into place, you can start to lead by letting go. You trust the people in your organization to implement the business, carrying out its functions under the guiding light of these visions and strategies. But first, you must assess how these strategic scenarios align with the whole of your business following the guidelines in the next chapter, before giving them the green light.

APPLYING SYSTAINERSHIP

Coaching Questions to Move Your Organization Toward Inventing Strategic Scenarios

1. What is the biggest challenge your company is facing today that could benefit from brainstorming new solutions and developing new horizons?
2. Who are the key visionaries and "imagineers" in your organization who could lead ideation sessions?
3. How could your integrated SEC team partner with these innovators to create new solutions?

For more coaching questions to help your business invent strategic scenarios, go to www.SustainableBusinessSystems.com/bq.

Call to Action

Work with your SEC team to identify and plan a pilot project to "imagineer" solutions to a current business challenge.

Your Insights on Inventing Strategic Scenarios

____

____

____

____

____

____

Moving Forward with the Systainership Function of Inventing Strategic Scenarios

What are five steps you can take now to lead your organization toward inventing strategic scenarios? Please list them in order of priority.

1. ______________________________________
2. ______________________________________
3. ______________________________________
4. ______________________________________
5. ______________________________________

CHAPTER

11

ALIGN YOUR BUSINESS ON A SUSTAINABLE COURSE

We are daily witnessing the phenomenon of the impossible of yesterday becoming the possible of today.

~ GANDHI (1869-1948)

A Mid-Course Correction—A Lesson from Interface, Inc.

In 1994, Interface, Inc.'s CEO, Ray Anderson, answered the question "are we on the right course?" with an astounding "no!"

Fueled by Paul Hawkins's words in *The Ecology of Commerce* and his inability to answer consumers' questions on how this carpet magnate was protecting the earth, Anderson realized his company wasn't fully in alignment. Although it seemed successful through 1995—sales exceeded $800 million and topped $1 billion in 1996 for the first time—Anderson sensed his company was headed on a gut-wrenching course of destruction.[84]

Interface started in 1973 in the industrial carpet business manufacturing modular carpet tiles. After years of acquisitions, it grew to include broadloom carpets, textiles, chemicals, and architectural products. For 21 years, the company was a good corporate citizen, complying with regulations. The simple act of reading Hawkins's book in 1994 set Anderson on a "mid-course correction," as he coined the phrase in his own book *Toward a Sustainable Enterprise: The Interface Model.*[85] How could Interface survive in the long run with products based on fossil fuels? How could it live with its participation in what Anderson believed to be the destruction of the earth?

That year, Anderson set out to make Interface a sustainable enterprise. During the first year of working toward triple-based profitability, he was bombarded with opinions from various experts on the earth's systems—from both alarmists and naysayers. He questioned his decision to go green that entire year, yet finally came to the same conclusion. He felt scientists on both sides were arguing that mankind was on a path toward the earth's destruction but on different time frames. Some said it will happen relatively soon, others that it's millenniums away. But even when Anderson compared millenniums to the earth's lifespan, he felt uneasy. After all, in less than a blink of the earth's eye, man discovered fossil fuels, revolutionized industry, and brought the earth "near" peril. For him, the exact time to reach destruction wouldn't matter; even a few millenniums are infinitesimal compared to the billions of years it took to create the earth.[86] In short, he believed something had to be done immediately.

Anderson upheld his mid-course correction decision using a three-pronged approach. First, Interface would establish an honest relationship with its customers, aligning with the goal of "doing well by doing good." This would paint a picture of a profitable company providing goods and services in a way that's good for the earth and its people.

Second, it would achieve resource efficiency by—

- minimizing what it takes from the earth.
- minimizing pollutants and toxins created through its processes.
- eliminating waste and creating a closed loop cycle.

This approach is based on both The Natural Step framework, developed collaboratively by Dr. Karl-Henrik Robèrt and 50 other scientists to define what's needed to sustain civilization on earth, and ideas from William McDonough and the Cradle-to-Cradle framework.

Third, it aimed to become an industry leader and set an example for other companies.[87]

Anderson knew getting from commitment to theoretical knowledge to working practice to teaching others would be a monumental undertaking, which he metaphorically called "climbing Mount Sustainability." Yet since 1994, Interface has progressed on all three fronts. It's been a rough road with many setbacks, but its leaders remain committed to climbing the mountain and leading the industry in sustainability.

Here are some of Interface's 2009 results as reported on its website:

- The company reduced the energy used to manufacture carpet by 43% since 1996.
- Greenhouse gas emissions are down 44% in absolute terms, or 94% when factoring in offsets, since 1996.
- Water intake per production unit is down 47% in broadloom carpet facilities and down 77% in modular carpet facilities.
- The percentage of recycled and bio-based materials used to manufacture its products worldwide has increased from less than 1% in 1996 to 36% in 2009.
- The cumulative avoided costs from waste elimination activities since 1995 are calculated to be over $433 million.[88]

Interface also established its consulting arm, InterfaceRAISE, which provides consultation to Walmart and other large corporations on sustainability initiatives.

Ray Anderson passed away in August 2011, leaving a legacy of commitment and passion for the ideal of sustainable businesses and a sustainable world. The ripple effect of his influence and inspiration has been for countless followers to take action.

GETTING INTO ALIGNMENT

No doubt you experience physical or emotional sensations when something in your world gets out of balance—just like your car pulls in strange ways when its front tire gets out of alignment. Similarly, when you commit to something you shouldn't have, feeling out of sorts may be evidenced as Sea Sweetleeder's burning in the pit of his stomach.

However, because of so many people and processes involved, it's hard to "feel" misalignments in business. Often, they're not recognized until after the company has traveled along the wrong path and hits an impasse.

How do you keep your business on the chosen course—fulfilling your mission and vision—while allocating resources and running it every day? Let's examine 14 approaches to achieving this.

14 APPROACHES TO CREATING BUSINESS ALIGNMENT

Within this Systainership function, you aim to align your organization at strategic and operational levels. You also extend traditional ROI analyses into other areas of business alignment. It's helpful to view alignment from the 14 approaches that follow.

Before examining each of your strategic scenarios, though, balance the makeup of your SEC team. Remember to have mostly left-brained analytical thinkers who thrive on logical, linear thinking and complement them with a few right-brain thinkers who will advocate for visionary strategic opportunities.

1. *Complete Scenarios*

   First, request that your team supplements the strategic scenarios from the previous function (in Chapter 10) with statements of impact, resources, logistics, etc. This is more aptly done by this analytical team than the visionaries who created the scenarios.

2. *Mission, Vision, and Values*

   In Chapter 5, you saw how to lead your company to create and articulate solid, sustainable mission, vision, and values statements.

Aligning with these is key to every project your organization undertakes. Why? Everything the company does supports the highest directives of the business. It facilitates getting buy-in to changes at all levels of the organization and makes implementation easier throughout.

Given that your company is constantly bombarded with challenges and opportunities, always check whether proposed actions, initiatives, or strategies move it toward its mission *in alignment with its vision and values.* Doing this helps remove the significance, enticement, fear, pain, apprehension, adventure, and array of other emotions attached to them while making the remaining alignment review more objective.

The stronger the alignment, the stronger the company will be and the simpler the whole process will become.

3. *Talents and Strengths*

Aligning new strategies with core business strengths puts any organization in a position of power. Talents can be augmented with outside sources if needed, although that's more advantageous in some organizational structures than others. When moving your organization in a new direction, look at this carefully. Know that when the strengths and talents available don't align well with those needed to execute a strategy, it increases the risks.

Alignment not only requires having the right talent; it's also a question of *how much* talent, *where* it's located, and *when* it can be allocated. And stretching your strengths too far can weaken them. Here are two simplified examples (looked at in the absence of other related factors) that show why it's important to prioritize how you apply the talents across your organizational strategies.

In the first example, a company has a low debt/equity ratio, positioning it well to request investment capital for pursuing new strategies. However, if several strategies require similar influxes of capital and raise the debt/equity ratio, the company's standing among investors and ability to raise capital in a critical situation could be jeopardized.

In the second example, a pharmaceutical company stands out

in its industry for its medical research. If the company adopts the strategy of developing affordable drugs for third-world countries while also adopting the strategy of researching a new line of drugs to treat cancer, its talent would be stretched too thin. Trying to rapidly expand the strength within the organization could weaken it, putting all new product development at risk. This shows why applying talents and strengths needs to be carefully planned.

4. *Return on Investment*

   In the traditional sense, a return on investment (ROI) analysis builds the financial case for prioritizing a company's strategies and projects. Sometimes these analyses result in sending good ideas back to the drawing board to reduce costs or accelerate gains within particular time frames.

   The ROI of sustainability strategies is analyzed similarly to any asset acquisition or use of venture capital. Company after company (including Interface) has demonstrated efficiencies and cost savings by implementing sustainable operations. Yet sustainable for-profit and nonprofit businesses—so important to the world—can't be sustainable themselves without a healthy economic platform. So look not only at what you're getting into but also what you're giving up in pursuing suggested sustainability strategies. They're your hidden costs.

5. *Allocation of Resources*

   Aligning resource allocation is needed for any strategy to succeed. This goes beyond the allocation of financial resources and human talents and includes facilities, equipment, materials availability, distribution, infrastructure, etc. All necessary resources need to be available within the correct timeframe and at particular locations. Plus all allocations must be balanced against the priorities of other business strategies.

   The sustainability of resources relates directly to the sustainability of your business, which is why transitioning to renewable resources must be considered when developing your strategies. Also consider leveraging your resources. Any resources you can share internally or externally within partnerships improve profitability, sustainability, and strategic timing. (This also relates to the discussion of systemic depth and breadth in #13.)

6. *Supporting Partnerships*

   Developing strategic partnerships to leverage resources and knowledge is important to your sustainability efforts. You may have already scoped out organizations with missions, visions, and values that align with yours. When evaluating new strategies, research desired partnerships and see how well certain projects could align with what those organizations are doing. Seek to strengthen existing partnerships through new projects. Always look for opportunities to create a strong web of partnerships.

   Remember, any alignment has to be mutually beneficial for the partnership to be strong. Take time to align timing and availability of resources across organizations before considering any partnership commitments and outline how each one can benefit. For example, the Hershey Company, presented in Chapter 4, undertakes many community and environmental stewardship projects in partnership with NGO organizations. This helps the company build its stewardship mission while protecting it from being the sole support of any community (which was a pitfall in its past).

7. *Organizational Sustainability*

   View every strategy and project through a sustainability lens, which requires going through a sustainability evaluation using current methodologies.

   For example, Interface used The Natural Step developed by 50 scientists under the direction of Dr. Karl-Henrik Robèrt. They developed a consensus on four conditions to define an environment that's not sustainable. That means, in becoming more sustainable, it's critical to *avoid* setting up these conditions:

   - Concentrations of substances extracted from the earth
   - Concentrations of substances produced by humans
   - Degradation of nature and natural processes
   - Creating conditions that systematically undermine the capacity of fellow humans to meet their needs

The Cradle to Cradle methodology presented by William McDonough and Michael Braungart in their book *Cradle to Cradle* challenges how products have historically been designed and manufactured. Since the Industrial Revolution, products have been produced linearly, taking resources from the earth and reformulating those into products that are eventually disposed of in landfills, incinerators, or other such "graves." In contrast, Cradle to Cradle production is a closed loop system producing only beneficial systemic byproducts (if they produce any at all). All spent production materials return to the system and are reused.

Another methodology, ISO 14000, was released by the International Organization for Standardization to help businesses reduce their environmental footprint and decrease waste and toxic emissions. Its systems and supporting audit guidelines focus primarily on "doing less bad," which can be a good starting point for some companies. The ISO 14000 system holds companies accountable to legal compliance and continued improvement.

You could raise the bar and set high goals for your company using The Natural Step or Cradle to Cradle with ISO 14000 as your accountability system. Among the other sustainability methodologies out there, you'll find one or a combination that fits your business.

The good news is that, in many areas, you won't have to reinvent the sustainability wheel. Industry best practices have been published by many large companies and certification programs in various industries. For a model, go to Interface's website at www.interfaceglobal.com. However, it is important to invent your own wheel in the areas that differentiate your business.

8. *Tipping Point*

Identify the biggest gap that your company needs to bridge to achieve exponential growth toward its vision of success, then examine how the proposed strategies will help to span that gap in a sustainable way. From there, assess which strategies will assist most in creating your company's tipping point.

For Interface, battling its waste issue generated significant funds to reinvest in other sustainability initiatives. On a smaller scale, the tipping point for independent entrepreneurs might be to adopt a strategy of delegation to free their own time and energy. That allows them to shift from working *in* the business to working *on* the business—and propelling it toward a sustainable future.

9. *Market and Brand Power*

The lifespan of your product or service is influenced by the position it enjoys in its marketplace and its brand recognition. Creating an uncontested market as described in the book *Blue Ocean Strategy* by W. Chan Kim and Renée Mauborgne might seem ideal. For most companies, that idealism isn't grounded in reality. However, dominating a market niche of considerable size and holding that position extends the viability of your company. Small companies that "went green" for ethical reasons found themselves enjoying a wide competitor-free market initially. However, many businesses in arenas with low entry barriers have joined the current drive for sustainability and now these markets have become quite competitive.

Relying on sustainability to differentiate your market loses its strength over time. As more businesses rise to the challenge of environmental and community stewardship, sustainability will become the norm, not the exception. The next measure will be not if your products are sustainable, but *how sustainable they are.* After that, customers will look for other differentiating characteristics in their buying choices.

> *Relying on sustainability to differentiate your market loses its strength over time.*

Any business strategy pursued will be stronger if it also aligns with strengthening brand recognition. For Interface, becoming sustainable has been embedded in its brand. It has emerged as an industry leader and holds that powerful brand recognition.

Similarly, your strategies should align with positioning your business in the best market possible. Implementing strategies that ensure your sustainability and strengthen the uniqueness of your brand within your market will serve you well.

10. *Organizational Timing*

Strategies and projects need to align with the timing of other events within your organization. Only a limited number of initiatives can be undertaken effectively and efficiently at any one time. Scattering both your focus and your resources too far weakens your organization.

Also consider contingencies. Look at how potential strategies relate to other existing or planned efforts within the organization, functionally or otherwise. Identify strategic dependencies and efforts that may be undertaken conditionally based on other outcomes. To set priorities, Interface identified how the faces of "Mount Sustainability" related to each other.

11. *Ease of Implementation*

Have you heard the expression "go for the low-hanging fruit"? This is the sustainability strategy for many companies. For some, it makes sense. But using a sustainable process to achieve sustainability will garner more success than from plucking the nearby fruit.

Examine your industry position and how quickly you can achieve change. Consider your market position and how to best maintain or grow it yet still reach your sustainable business model goals. After all, you don't want your company busy switching incandescent light bulbs to CFSs when your primary competitor is enrolling its customers into sustainable partnerships, attracting new ones, and creating deeper loyalty. If you go for the low-hanging fruit, you could be moving your company toward greater sustainability in one arena at the expense of another.

On the other hand, all things being equal, choosing strategies that are easy to implement or fast to complete could give the whole organization a confidence boost. It could improve company morale and increase employee alignment, providing additional benefits. So an immediate return on investment might not be as powerful as other strategies, but it could be used to test the waters in new arenas.

12. Technological Developments

Is your technology keeping up with the vision you hold for your company? Perhaps you're ahead of the curve and need vertical integration to develop new technology that will support your growth. Some industries simply bide time until new technologies appear. For example, electricity generation and automobile manufacture will both be significantly affected by technological developments in energy storage. Other companies are on the forefront of technological advances looking for industry applications.

Examine how your strategies are affected by technological advances and vice versa. Be aware that aligning with technologies that maintain or improve your market position strengthens the sustainability of your company. Aligning with sustainable technologies further strengthens its sustainability.

If your technology needs can't be met within your timeframe, consider strategies you can implement as stopgap measures. Carefully assess any urgency for your company to be on the forefront of technological advances.

13. Systemic Depth and Breadth

Often strategies are assessed in a compartmentalized way along functional, geographical, product, or market lines. Increase benefits by looking for connectivity across these imposed boundaries, or you might discover benefits resulting from expanding a strategy the full length of a silo. In fact, strategies that are systemic offer more benefits and therefore have greater importance than other strategic scenarios. Remember, you always want to leverage your resources to the max.

14. Risk Assessment

Some of the 13 strategic alignment sections touch on associated areas of risks that include complexity, large capital investments, inexperience, technology, reputation, unpredictable markets, opportunity loss, competition, etc. The point is not to ignore risk assessment but rather to make complete risk assessment part of any strategic scenario alignment you undertake.

THE SYSTAINERSHIP FUNCTION OF ASSESSING SUSTAINABILITY ALIGNMENT

The function of visioning sustainable strategic scenarios (in Chapter 10) asked you to lead your visionaries to create strategic scenarios that provide innovative solutions to the challenges and opportunities your organization faces. These were created with a mix of imaginative abandon and focused direction. Now it's time to pull back on the reins. When assessing alignment for sustainability, these strategic scenarios must be evaluated for their alignment with *where the organization is, where it wants to be, and how it will get there*. The strength of this alignment correlates to strengthening the sustainability of your organization. The function guides you to the numerous viewpoints from which alignment is considered. Figure 12 indicates how this alignment function is integrated into the entire system.

Because there's no such thing as perfect alignment, you'll make tradeoffs when planning your company's pathways.

Because there's no such thing as perfect alignment, you'll make tradeoffs when planning your company's pathways. Again—under the guidance of the mission, vision, and values, and the organization's areas of focus and strategic tiers—you can proceed to approve and schedule the most aligned strategies for your business.

SUSTAINABILITY BENEFITS THROUGH ASSESSING SUSTAINABILITY ALIGNMENT

Strategic alignment is a powerful practice that promotes sustainability at each of the five levels discussed in Chapter 3. As you execute this function, your company selects the most viable strategic scenarios that will support your business mission, vision, and values as well as make the most of its talents and strengths and provide for the biggest return on investment. You're prioritizing your strategies to maximize the allocation of company resources. You synchronize your strategies with

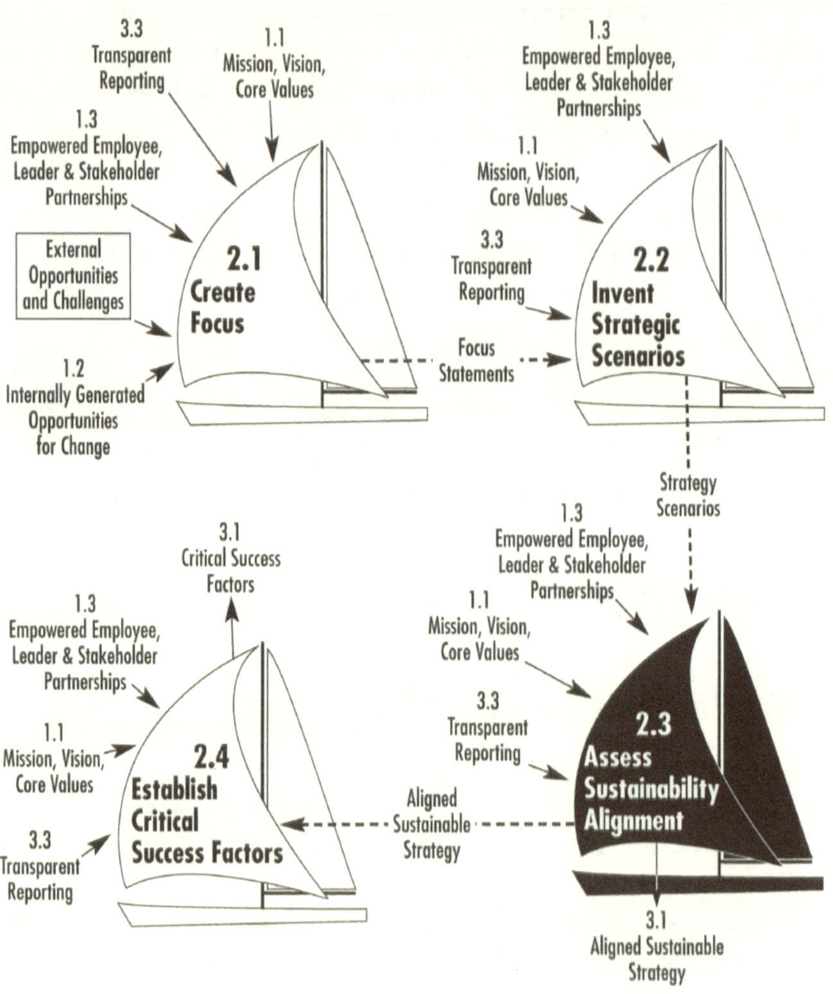

Figure 12

your strategic partners to allow you to effectively leverage resources in a compatible timeframe.

You evaluate every strategy through a sustainability lens, ensuring business practices that uphold your responsibility as a steward of the environment and society, while at the same time these aligned strategies gain momentum on the road to triple-based profitability.

APPLYING SYSTAINERSHIP

Coaching Questions to Move Your Organization Toward Assessing Sustainability Alignment

1. What current strategy is your company struggling with most?
2. How sustainable is that strategy?
3. What would pull that strategy into greater alignment with your company and accelerate success?

For more coaching questions to help your business assess sustainability alignment, go to www.SustainableBusinessSystems.com/bq.

Call to Action

With your SEC team, pick a key area of alignment for your business and design an alignment measurement system for evaluating future projects. (If you're just starting out, keep it simple.)

Your Insights on Assessing Sustainability Alignment

____

____

____

____

____

____

Moving Forward with the Systainership Function of Assessing Sustainability Alignment

What are five steps you can take now to lead your organization toward assessing sustainability alignment? Please list them in order of priority.

1. ____
2. ____
3. ____
4. ____
5. ____

CHAPTER

12

PLOT YOUR POSITION WITH APPROPRIATE MEASURES

We are drowning in information but starved for knowledge.

~ JOHN NAISBITT (1929-)

A Mission-driven Bank Defines Sustainable Success—A Lesson from ShoreBank Pacific

ShoreBank Pacific started as the brainchild of Spencer Beebe of Eco-Trust, who developed the concept with ShoreBank Corp. of Chicago. The concept was to help local bank customers grow their businesses in a way that would promote stewardship of the environment, social community, and economic development. The partnership resulted in the formation of ShoreBank Pacific, which opened its doors in Ilwaco, Washington in 1997.[89] They expanded into two additional physical locations in Washington and Oregon while a growing percentage of their customers enjoy its online banking services from remote regions.

From 2000 through 2008, the bank's net income almost doubled annually. During 2008, loans grew 25% to exceed $110 million, deposits grew 28% to almost $148 million, and total assets increased 10 fold to exceed $200 million.[90] This success comes out of the founders' mission to help business owners while being good stewards of the environment and communities in which they operate.

But how does the bank know if it's on "solid ground" and achieving its mission?

To meet that need, ShoreBank Pacific developed nine evaluation criteria for determining the level of sustainability of any of its loan customers. These criteria address company stewardship of the environment, society, and economic development.

There are three sustainability ratings in each area. Each of the nine is rated from 0 to 3, based on whether the business practices executed in a particular area are conventional (0), business-as-usual (1), sustainable (2), or demonstrating effective, innovative practices (3).[91] A perfect mission score would be 27 with a top rating of 3 in each of the nine areas. The bank continues to increase the mission scores of its loan portfolio's aggregate rating with complete transparency. It uses the same evaluation method to report its own progress and includes this within its sustainability report developed under the framework of the Global Reporting Initiative.

The nine criteria for assessing businesses and making loan decisions are based on the four guiding principles of The Natural Step (described in Chapter 11). The underlying levels of information roll up to this loan portfolio decision layer. The bank uses these underlying layers to communicate with and educate its clients on relevant sustainability issues.[92] Its staff continually works with them to improve their practices and mission scores over the life of their loan.

In Appendix A of its 2006 Sustainability Report,[93] the bank stated its goal as having 80% of its loan clients' mission scores rated at 6 or higher based on the aggregate loan dollars. Although its 2007-2008 Sustainability Report doesn't state the same goal, it reflects nearly 70% of outstanding loan dollars to companies with a mission score of 6 or higher for 2008. ShoreBank Pacific was coming ever closer to its earlier goal of 80% when economic tides turned!

In July of 2009, the FDIC declared ShoreBank Pacific's parent company "engaged in unsafe or unsound banking practices" and closed ShoreBank Corp. on August 20, 2010. The corporation had been on a downhill trend with a $9.3 million loss in 2008, a $119 million loss in 2009, and a loss of $39.6 million for the first half of 2010.[94] However, ShoreBank Pacific was not part of the FDIC takeover. Due to its solid capital levels and equity ratio, it was not included in the federal seizure. The very next day, ShoreBank Pacific announced a merger with the San Francisco-based OneCalifornia Bank. Today, it continues its mission-driven community bank focus as One PacificCoast Bank.[95]

As you see from ShoreBank Pacific's story, its well-defined critical success factors served them well. Its criteria convey how well a company is performing on its journey and when it's reached its destination. In the bank's system, the ultimate goal is a score of 27 (achieving level 3 in each of the nine categories) based on multiple underlying layers of triple-based reporting. This story might inspire you to create your own critical success factors based on your company's focal areas of business.

Exactly what are critical success factors? Like the instrument panel of a ship indicating its status at sea, they provide key indicators that communicate the status of your business in different areas. (Chapter 16 addresses nuances of reporting these factors transparently.) It's necessary to know how to develop critical success factors that can help you guide your business to sustainable success.

9 CONSIDERATIONS IN ESTABLISHING CRITICAL SUCCESS FACTORS

Here are nine considerations for establishing critical success factors appropriate for your business.

1. *Provide Data that Promotes Trust*

   Vested parties are interested in the financial status plus the social and environmental stewardship of your businesses. Many companies participate in transparent reporting to communicate their achievements. However, a lot of these reports leave the reader with more questions than answers when they fail to use sufficient and reliable data. Because the data is often voluminous and confusing without industry standards, third-party organizations developed certifications as a shortcut for consumers to understand what the organization has achieved in its stewardship areas. But having a plethora of certifications without any standards across them can still be confusing. Over time, this certification process is becoming insufficient and unreliable. Companies that develop data strategies to meet these certifications are doing themselves a disservice when other critical success factors are more important for gauging their own progress.

   The data used to create any reporting must be trustworthy because their value is felt throughout the business's circle of influence. Reporting of data directly affects building and maintaining partnerships—from employees to stockholders and from customers to vendors. Certainly any partnership aligned with your mission will be negatively affected by the presence of any misleading data, intentional or not. Any claims made should be backed by data that can be verified. Details of the data don't have to be part of the message but must be available to substantiate your message through websites, reports, or other means.

2. *Reflect Your Related Experience and Knowledge*

   According to Joel Makower, author of *Strategies for the Green Economy*, relevant information starts with data about what you know and expands to include data about what you're doing about what you know.[96] Taking that direction, you would tailor your model to fit your goals and the legacy you're striving for. You'd use your success factors to represent the level of learning and achievement you have attained. The model you create and how you communicate your achievements further differentiate you in the marketplace. You want your message seen as honest and humble while still speaking to your mission and showing your credibility. Communicating your success factors will help to uphold your business in the marketplace as "green/sustainable" becomes mainstream. Not far in the future, the question becomes not one of whether your company is sustainable, but in what ways has it become sustainable and what measures demonstrate that. A certification may be just one of the measures that fits your company.

3. *Be Specific and Measurable*

Striving for greater sustainability is a noble goal, but how will you know when your company has achieved it? Is it just a "little more" improvement that you want? Or are you looking for "significant" improvement? Being specific and measurable allows you to efficiently evaluate your progress and communicate it to others, both internally and externally. Bottom lines for the new horizons of your business need to be as specific and measurable as your traditional financial bottom lines. When statements of qualitative happenings versus quantitative measures result in head scratching, you know your communication is ineffective. It's also true no one can distinguish results relative to the scale of an organization from most qualitative measures. Even some quantitative measures out of context aren't helpful.

Organizations can develop their own new bottom lines based on the knowledge and practical demands of their operations. They can then use these elements as communication tools to enroll their stakeholders in operations and partnerships key to the future of the business, the environment, and the communities. Indeed, without this information, motivation dwindles and progress is hindered.

Some say all this "stuff" just isn't measurable. I contend that, in most cases, you can drill down beneath the qualitative activities to find quantitative measures supporting those activities. You can also tailor the measures to the size and direction of your organization, making them practical and effective.

Tracking progress in the area of community support and stakeholder citizenship seems to be the hardest to grasp. How do you measure employee engagement, customer loyalty, supplier partnerships, stockholder enrollment, community development, and that kind of "stuff"? Let's address employee engagement as an example. Say the two factors involved are (1) establishing corporate culture programs and (2) employee safety. To have both of these on the rise could be good for your company and demonstrate employee engagement. The employee engagement might then be measured this way:

number of corporate culture programs × percent of employee participation ÷ number of employee accidents/total employee hours

(Note: For the mathematical purists, in the case of 0 accidents, because dividing by zero is not possible, a minute value would have to be included in the divisor. Surely someone must have put a band-aid on a paper cut to count as one micro-accident!)

As the number of programs increases, employee engagement increases. As the percent of employee participation increases, so does this measure of employee engagement. As accidents increase, the employee engagement indicator decreases. As the total hours increase, this factor increases. One company might want to include turnover as a parameter; another might want to use this as the critical success factor affecting turnover; a third might find its turnover ratio a sufficient and effective measure in place of this algorithm. Any number of parameters could be considered.

Important in creating *any* critical success factor is knowing what it means for the business at the level it's being used. And it should indicate progress, supported by solid underlying data. Any critical success factor used by the CEO and other top executives must also have a defined level at which the company can operate sustainably. Achievements beyond that are regenerative!

4. *Cite Areas of Business Focus*

The financial leg of the triple-based approach has had institutions guarding its fair and equitable reporting since the first system was documented in 1494 by Fr. Luca Paciolo, an Italian monk and mathematician. This system still forms the basis of what's used today, although it's been modernized significantly over the last few centuries.[97]

More recent reporting movements include government compliance. The EPA and various governments have set legal limits for how "non-green" an entity can be while OSHA has set standards for safety. Clearly, these and other government agencies define boundaries and oversee their compliance.

But are these the sustainable bottom lines that define success for the future of your company? Which, if any of these, relate to the focus areas of your business?

The critical success factors selected must correspond to areas of business focus. (Chapter 9 discussed areas of focus.) Many traditional financial bottom lines are calculated and tracked, but companies generally focus on the few that support the strategic initiatives underway (and their detailed supporting success factors).

Kaplan and Norton introduced the concept of linking strategies to performance measures and expounded on this approach in their 1996 book *The Balanced Scorecard: Translating Strategy Into Action*. They made these links in four areas:

- Employee learning and growth
- Internal business performance
- Customer satisfaction
- Financial performance

You can approach triple-based profitability strategies pertaining to an area of focus similarly. These strategies may involve success factors related to one, two, or all three areas of stewardship—financial, social, and/or environmental.

At operational levels, selecting the right critical success factors that serve to inform and motivate without overwhelming people is required. As an example, to evaluate their loan clients, the founders of ShoreBank Pacific selected nine success factors with a simple scale to communicate a client's level of sustainability to the loan portfolio managers. The layers of supporting data the bank receives from its clients would be confusing and overwhelming to those evaluating the sustainability of the bank's loan portfolio. However, they'd be helpful in validating their customers' progress and conducting consultations when striving to understand how they are moving forward with specific strategies.

Developing sustainable businesses proactively with appropriate critical success factors will give government agencies *less reason* to impose additional compliance rules and provide *more flexibility* in generating sustainable practices that align with your business.

5. *Measure in Context*

So what does it mean to say a company has recycled 50 tons of cardboard or 100% of it? If the 50 tons indicate 10 more tons than the previous year, but the amount of manufactured product increased by 30%, then the company's recycling efficiency went down. And which is more sustainable—a large company recycling 50 tons of cardboard, or a small mom-and-pop business recycling 100% of its cardboard? Admittedly, it's hard to determine progress with these types of figures.

Norton and Kaplan, creators of the Balanced Scorecard, suggested combining information or giving additional background information to put the measures in context. In Systainership, context is built into your measures. Examples of measuring in context from traditional financial measures include:

- Sales are generally measured over time with the profit margin as a percentage of sales.
- Return on equity is profits measured against the value of equity as a percentage.
- The debt/equity ratio measures level of debt against the level of equity.
- The dividend yield is per share, and so forth.

When you start measuring environmental and social bottom lines against operational units of context, you'll start to see true progress toward sustainability.

Combining this kind of data with what you know leads to more meaningful data for your business and stakeholders. Look at which social and environmental bottom lines make sense for your business. Determine a meaningful context in which they should be measured and what impact those measurements could have on your stakeholders.

6. *Create Data That's Relevant*

While I was a graduate student at Harvard, I took a consulting course at the Harvard Business School as part of my multi-disciplined curriculum. With a classmate, we helped our client, Federal Judicial Center in Washington, DC, and specifically its IT department (as it's called now). At the Center, people schedule, monitor, and track all federal cases and related federal court activity, making the performance of its computer system critical to upholding justice for the whole country.

The Judicial Center had many reports showing the status and performance of the various components of their systems, but the judicial managers couldn't understand the technical implications. My partner and I, removed from their everyday activities, were able to think "outside the box" to create solutions. Specifically, we designed a series of reports for non-technical management based on balance algorithms that showed the system performance, capacity, and utilization as geometric shapes based on the number of parameters. If five parameters were involved in performance, then the resulting report would be a pentagon. If the pentagon was perfectly shaped, the system was in balance. If it wasn't, the sides that weren't proportional were easily identified and so were the specific performance issues. You could also overlay historical shapes to see growth. I conceived the model for this and my partner determined the feasibility of the algorithms. People at the Federal Judicial Center were so delighted with the concept we created, they offered each of us a job!

Naturally, all information has to relate to its intended audience. So when establishing critical success factors, they must be gauged to the level people will use them so they don't get overwhelmed. Remember, your goal is to always create understanding and motivation. Critical success factors used for evaluating performance should have all supporting factors under the control of the unit being evaluated.

7. *Escalate Organizational Enrollment*
   Achieving the sustainability levels of your organization's critical success factors depends on the performance of everyone within your organization who contributes to it. When established properly, these success factors link to the organization's mission, create motivation, and further the understanding, through the roll up process, of how individual performance contributes to the overall goals. Creating awareness of this throughout the organization will increase employees' resolve for achievement. To fortify that resolve, provide proper training in how the critical success factors will be established, interpreted, and integrated into the operations so employees can competently incorporate them into their work. In turn, this awareness, training, and competence will empower employees to achieve greater success than ever.

8. *Evaluate the Cost of Data Collection*
   All information has a price tag and so does lack of information or inadequate information in terms of risk. This causes you to constantly weigh the trade-offs between the value of information and its cost. Some can be obtained easily and inexpensively while others are complex and costly. Be sure to consider these trade-offs when creating the methods of measuring your critical success factors.

   Another consideration is your current stage of business development. For small new businesses, it may be more practical to use estimates than do the detailed data capturing and reporting that large companies use. Most likely, ShoreBank Pacific's underlying levels of data have become more sophisticated over time as their clients have grown, developed, and become more sustainable. You can see an evolution of their information in their sustainability reports.

9. *Set Up a Monitoring System*

Once your critical success factors have been determined at all levels of your organization, you'll determine the data-capturing and reporting systems needed to monitor your progress. These systems will need to fit into the ongoing operations of the business. They'll gather, transfer, and store measurements necessary to calculate the critical success factors. They'll also interface with operational systems and may require data sensors. More sophisticated systems provide data authentication; some require authorization to input or extract data.

These systems also need to be tailored to the size of your organization, your level of business development, and the resources available. They can be as simple as weighing all your waste or as complex as measuring the number of parts per million by volume of sulfur molecules released into the atmosphere. When using estimates or other non-specific measures, be sure to disclose the method along with the information to maintain integrity and transparency. The level of monitoring also relates to what you know about the sustainability initiatives of your business. As you progress along your journey and your learning expands, so will the sophistication of your monitoring systems, if needed.

THE SYSTAINERSHIP FUNCTION OF ESTABLISHING CRITICAL SUCCESS FACTORS

In this Systainership function, you lead your organization to determine the best critical success factors each time new sustainable strategies are approved. Refer to Figure 13.

Each success factor must be specific and measurable, relevant to the organizational level, and based on the business's sustainability model.

Your company, working with participating business partners, evaluates each sustainable strategy to determine how success will be defined and how it will effectively motivate those who carry out the strategy. Critical

Systainership™

2.4 Establish Critical Success Factors

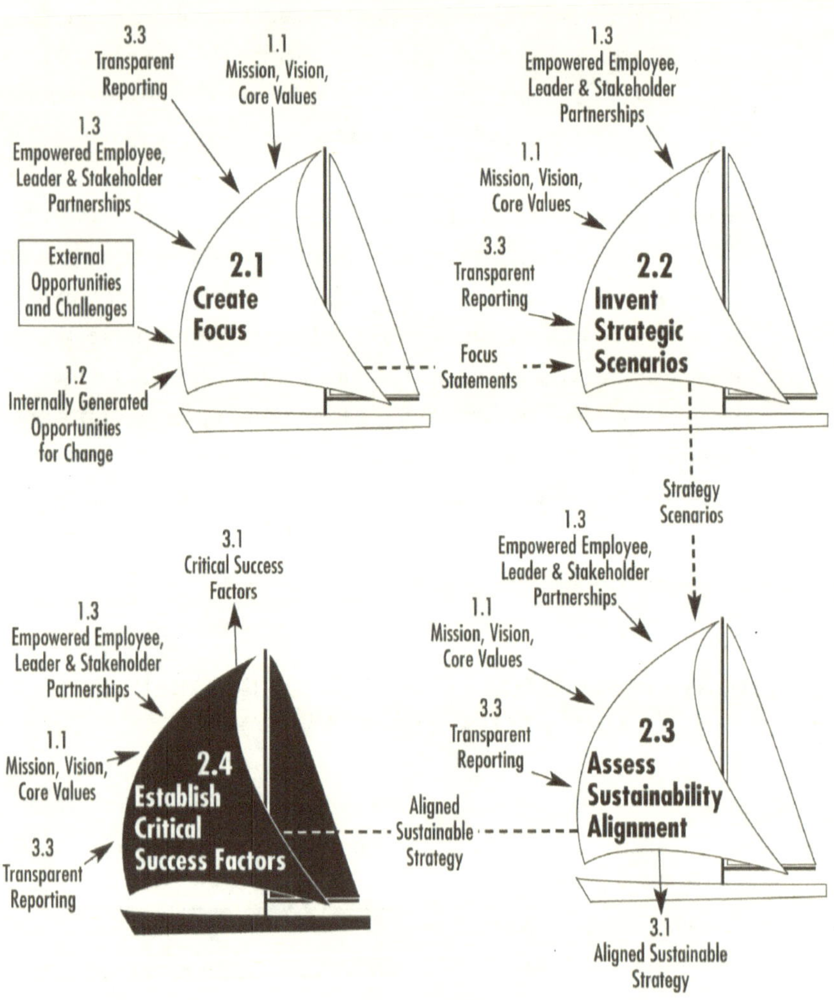

Figure 13

success factors are then evaluated and changed based on how well they support the business's areas of focus.

Each success factor must be specific and measurable, relevant to the organizational level, and based on the business's sustainability model. Looking at how the information can be provided, you make trade-offs involving the value, cost, and confidence level of information that will benefit the business. This gets forwarded to the next function of developing sustainable systems in which the stated information requirements become part of the operational systems.

SUSTAINABILITY BENEFITS THROUGH ESTABLISHING CRITICAL SUCCESS FACTORS

Leading your organization in establishing critical success factors is key to achieving triple-based profitability. These factors communicate progress on your company that's meaningful, trustworthy, and relevant to your business. They also relate to the economic, social, and environmental sustainability of your business. As such, they're contributing factors to the sustainability of the world as well. Establishing them helps your organization stay focused in executing its strategy, achieving its goals, and moving forward on its sustainable journey.

I suggest you tailor critical success factors to the size and development of your business so they're beneficial, not burdensome. When designed for each level of the organization, they provide motivation and direction while moving the organization toward greater sustainability.

Choosing factors *based on your own business model* will support your business legacy and further differentiate you in your marketplace—thus increasing sustainability. The right success factors lend authenticity to information conveyed to stakeholders and further empower partnerships. For employees, relevant success factors create greater dedication and loyalty. For customers, they

The right success factors lend authenticity to information conveyed to stakeholders and further empower partnerships.

create greater credibility that leads to increased sales. For stockholders, they increase the perception of competence and alignment resulting in increased confidence.

Critical success factors are indeed critical to your business's success!

APPLYING SYSTAINERSHIP

Coaching Questions to Move Your Organization Toward Establishing Critical Success Factors

1. How much information do you have to sift through to know how well your company is achieving its overall goals?
2. In what ways do your frontline workers see their performance contributing to the company's overall goals?
3. How much trust do your stakeholders have in your company's triple-based profitability reporting?

For more coaching questions to help your business establish critical success factors, go to www.SustainableBusinessSystems.com/bq.

Call to Action

Pick a key business strategy that doesn't have an appropriate critical success factor, design one, and determine appropriate layers of organizational supporting data that will roll into it.

Your Insights on Establishing Critical Success Factors

____

____

____

____

____

____

Moving Forward with the Systainership Function of Establishing Critical Success Factors

What are five steps you can take now to lead your organization toward establishing critical success factors? Please list them in order of priority.

1. ______________________________
2. ______________________________
3. ______________________________
4. ______________________________
5. ______________________________

PART FOUR

Making Headway

A good intention but fixed and resolute—
bent on high and holy ends,
we shall find means to them
on every side and at every moment;
and even obstacles and opposition will but
make us "like the fabled specter-ships,"
which sail the fastest
in the very teeth of the wind.

~ RALPH WALDO EMERSON (1803-1882)

CHAPTER

13

UNDERWAY WITH YOUR SUSTAINABILITY

We are living in a time when
mastering change is probably the most important
thing that leaders can help their organizations do.

~ ROSABETH MOSS KANTER (1943-)

A City in Trouble Transforms—A Lesson from Taipei

Taipei, Taiwan, with more than 2.6 million people living in 105 square miles, is one of the most densely populated cities in the world—nearly 25,000 people per square mile.[98] Plagued with high levels of air, water, and noise pollution, it spews out an unmanageable amount of solid and toxic waste for the environment to absorb. The city's dense mass of buildings, limited parklands, and vast areas of asphalt increase air temperatures and prevent high volumes of rainfall from being absorbed into the ground.[99] This is important because the city has three rivers and is surrounded by mountains on three sides so torrential rains during typhoon season pose dangerous flooding threats every year.[100]

From 1994 to 2006, Taipei's leaders took numerous steps to make the city more sustainable. In 2006, 51 sustainability indicators were developed to assess its progress and statistical data was collected to identify trends. During those 11 years, the 51 indicators showed that social and environmental efforts improved while economic and institutional efforts reflected poorly. Yet even with sustainability falling behind in some areas, the city's overall performance tended toward increased sustainability.[101] From 2006 to 2008, the 51 indicators were reduced to 41. From 2007 to 2008, 27 indicators showed the city steering toward greater sustainability while 11 show it deviated further away.

In 2009, Taipei's leaders felt uneasy with the oscillating progress and decided to quicken the pace of reaching a sustainable future. The new effort has been named Taipei Eco City. Bob Wise, director of Team Oregon, LLC, worked with the city and its various partner organizations to develop a new vision and action plan to realize a more sustainable future.

Taipei has now adopted a vision of sustainability for 2050 with interim visions for 2010 and 2015. The vision for 2050 is this: "Taipei is a living, restorative urban organism that sustains itself from the solar, wind, water and geothermal income and natural endowments. The city is like a tree with its vitality based on the resource derived from the place where it has deep roots. It provides 21st-century innovative living and organic solutions emphasizing the disciplines of systems science, biological and ecological sciences, bio mimicry, green chemistry, microbiology, materials science and other related fields."[102]

City leaders are taking a strong position to address both local and global challenges, including the reduction of greenhouse gas emissions as supported by The Natural Step (TNS) framework and the UN Green Cities Declaration. The Taipei Sustainable Development Committee, working through the TNS process, has classified issues in six sustainability categories: nature, water, energy, infrastructure, people, and their connectivity to global communities.[103]

Planning under the TNS framework, the city adopted new ways to improve and augment existing systems in each of these six areas. Governments are set up for volumes of citizens, officials, and employees to flow through their systems and conduct its "business." Indeed, its efficiency and effectiveness depend on the high quality of these systems.

Taipei is replacing its traditional bureaucracy with systems that support its sustainable vision. To design these changes, they used the TNS back casting approach. Using this process, organizational planners virtually sit in its future existence and look back to the present. They determine at each step backward what needs to change and how to accomplish those changes.

In the past, government systems have been established by reacting to conditions rather than proactively developing systems under a guiding vision. As they create new visions of sustainable coexistence, though, Taipei and other cities and governments are actively addressing not only the needs of their populace but also the need to support the earth's system. The Taipei Eco City vision addresses the environmental, social, and economic initiatives to bridge the gap from where the city is today and where its leaders want it to be by 2050. The people and government of Taipei are setting up new systems under new guidelines. By working in this framework, they know exactly what the success they have envisioned looks like and can move forward with resolve.

You, too, can apply the lessons of Taipei to your business.

INTEGRATING SUSTAINABLE PRACTICES

Having set your course by following ideas in the previous chapters, you're on track to create your sustainable enterprise. It's time for leaders in your organization to let go of the reins and empower those who are creating and implementing the business changes to support the adopted sustainable business strategies.

The city of Taipei example illustrates the first of three leadership functions necessary to propel your organization into sustainable operations—systemization—followed in the next three chapters by momentum and transparency.

When integrating sustainable business practices, you transition from planning to practice as you undertake operational changes to support, drive, and monitor the new strategies. You've made sure the proposed changes completely align with the organization and its stakeholders; your organizational culture has been primed to be adept at change. With your company being ready to operate more sustainably, your leadership role adapts to this phase.

CREATING SUCCESS THROUGH HONING YOUR SYSTEMS

Systemization sets up your company for repeatable success. It takes the guesswork out of what needs to be done, who should do it, how it's to be done, and what the tolerances are. In short, systems show how to execute winning strategies. Honing your systems is important to the overall success of your organization. As an example, from their 2006 initiative to their 2008 results, Taipei city leaders determined that their initial vision was lacking, progress was insufficient, and a greater thrust was needed.

Systemization sets up your company for repeatable success.

In 2009, a stronger vision for EcoCity Taipei was adopted under new guidance from Team Oregon, LLC, directed by Bob Wise. One example area of improvement was recycling. Taipei already had an extensive recycling program but, through this new effort, the leaders upped their goal to zero landfill and total recycling by 2010. By 2009 year end, it was apparent they weren't going to reach this goal. However, they reported an impressive 60% reduction in trash, and they're moving forward with more improvements.[104]

As you listen to the voices around you, you'll hear the frustrations of incorporating the sustainable strategies into your core business practices. Your response is to strive to connect relevant knowledge and resources throughout the company to achieve those improvements. Don't let up. Keep asking, "How could we improve this system to handle that issue better?"

Also, I suggest leading by example in systematizing what you do. Let go of your domain; systematize and *delegate.* (Read more about systemization in Chapter 14.) Doing this across the organization increases overall productivity, makes operations more sustainable, and propels everyone toward achieving your organization's vision.

ACCELERATING FORWARD THROUGH STAKEHOLDER MOMENTUM

Leadership transforms when your operations people take over and execute the changes and systems that will drive the adopted strategic plan. As a leader, you ensure that momentum builds by fortifying their efforts and reaching for a tipping point in these ways:

- Keep the vision and interconnectedness of the strategies alive for every individual within the organization requires an intentional, concentrated internal communications campaign.
- Pull stories out of your back pocket and speak in inclusive terms, talking about "we" not "I."
- Set aside time to dialogue with people in your organization and within your industry as well as non-industry partners.
- Set up monitoring systems to provide data needed to evaluate critical success factors.
- Deliver relevant, appropriate messages that keep all stakeholders informed.
- Provide feedback and transparency as a way to hone honest, loyal relationships.

TRANSPARENT COMMUNICATION PROVIDES CONNECTEDNESS

After evaluating their first efforts, Taipei's leaders found the city falling short in critical areas. To their credit, they published online yearly

Systainership™

3. Generate Sustainable Momentum

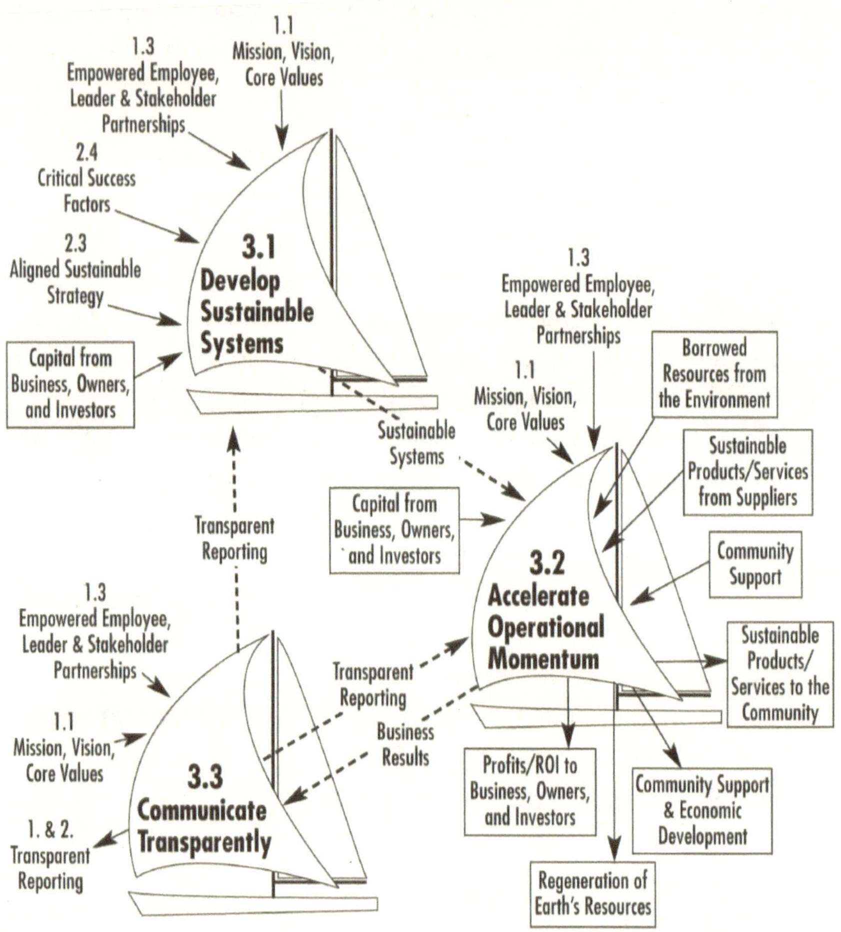

Figure 14

progress reports so they'd be seen by all stakeholders and the populace at large. Officials publicly admitted their initiatives weren't advancing as anticipated and announced a plan to regroup. After regrouping, they published a more sustainability-driven approach for the world to see. This transparency and willingness to take corrective action has endeared the city to the hearts of many.

The following three chapters build on the model noted in Figure 14. They describe the leaders' role in integrating sustainable business practices in these key areas:

- Develop sustainable systems.
- Accelerate operational momentum.
- Communicate transparently.

Common to each is to first listen and then recognize needs, lead by example, and facilitate connections. Master these ideas and your company will be on its way to a more sustainable future. Then, when you're ready for the next phase, you'll move further toward your triple-based profitability goals with grace, ease, and adeptness.

CHAPTER

14

REPLICATE SUSTAINABLE SUCCESS

If you can't describe what you are doing as a process, you don't know what you are doing.

~ W. EDWARDS DEMING (1900-1993)

Drive-through Sustainability—A Lesson from McDonald's

Is this an oxymoron? Can fast food be sustainable?

In 1994, Dr. Karl-Henrik Robèrt, founder of TNS (The Natural Step discussed in Chapter 11), introduced its principles to Mats Lederhausen, the new managing director of McDonald's Sweden. Over the next few years, McDonald's Sweden conducted training courses that introduced thousands of employees to the business principles of sustainability.[105] They started with recycling, organic procurement, phasing out plastics, and generating renewable energy. By 1998, the company had realized extensive cost savings through eco-efficiency programs, transformed its public image, and energized and motivated its staff. Lederhausen discovered that meaningful work brought out the best in his employees and they found meaning in the work they were doing toward building a sustainable society.[106]

McDonald's Sweden served as an example for other divisions of McDonald's. Lederhausen went to McDonald's corporate headquarters in Chicago and proposed to do for the rest of McDonald's what he had done for McDonald's Sweden. He became the head of global strategy and president of business development, influencing sustainable changes within the McDonald's Corporation for four years.[107] This company excels in systematizing its operations, and their sustainability efforts followed suit.

Today, its 31,000 restaurants operate worldwide with about 75% of them independently owned.[108] McDonald's is ranked 26th on *Newsweek*'s 2009 Top 500 Green U.S. Companies, leading in the media, travel, leisure industry sector for extending environmental stewardship to the ends of its supply chain.[109]

McDonald's success has stemmed from upholding its four core values through systematization: quality, service, cleanliness, and value. When Ray Kroc bought the franchise in 1955, he developed systematization in all aspects of the business—from the management of the restaurants through operations—to *consistently* deliver these values to the customer. And he opened its Hamburger University to train new franchise owners in these systems.[110]

Does systematization imply company stagnancy or antiquated systems? Certainly not. Over the years, McDonald's has continually expanded and honed its systems for greater efficiency, productivity, and profitability. Over the last decade, these systems have been further expanded to support greater sustainability.

Plus its new sustainability systems extend to its massive supply chain and communities in which its franchises and company stores operate. These systems include animal welfare audits, Flagship Farms in Europe to design and share best sustainable agricultural practices, Supplier Quality Management System, Code of Conduct for Suppliers, global packaging scorecard, Ronald McDonald House Charities and others.[111]

In pursuing sustainability, this global company found that certain sustainability issues need local solutions. In testing sustainability systems in different countries—for example, solar hot water heating in Mexico, recycled cooking oil in Brazil for biodiesel processors, a water conservation system in Australia, an EcoProgress energy efficiency software system in France—McDonald's researchers found that not all solutions are transportable to geographically diverse locations. Today, they work to develop solutions appropriate to regional characteristics. Best practices that improve productivity, resource efficiencies, sustainability, and profitability are then systematized and distributed throughout regions with similar conditions.

THE IMPORTANCE OF SYSTEMIZATION

The importance of systemization in business has been espoused by the famed professor, statistician, and business consultant W. Edwards Deming. He's been credited as a key player who helped Japan turn its economy around after World War II. Following Deming's success, many U.S. businesses opted to follow his approach. His teachings regarding the creation of systems to achieve production with a quality focus have been adopted worldwide.

Deming's quotation that opens this chapter says that people don't know what they're doing unless they can describe it as a process. Describing processes allows what's being done to be systematized, taught to others, replicated, and standardized. Why? To increase productivity and efficiency thus contributing to sustainability and profitability. Further, new operations designed specifically to create greater sustainability for a company will benefit in the same way from systemization, maximizing these efforts.

Think of the system called "democracy" as what led to the American Revolution. On its heels, systemization in production created the Industrial Revolution. Systemization of information created the Information Age. Today, systems are being combined to create the Connected Age, made possible by internet advancements.

The Connected Age is building relationships among people, information, disciplines, organizations, and more. They're linking values, sharing resources, combining perspectives, contributing to mutual benefit, and raising consciousness. In fact, contributing to the sustainability of the world is part of and also driven by the Connected Age. As the McDonald's story shows, the success of its initial systems supporting its business values led its leaders to create even more sustainable business systems supporting more sustainable business practices. In a similar vein, many companies are developing additional systems to help sustain both business and the earth.

Systemization leads to success by making successful operations replicable. This is the basis for the creation of franchises. It's also the basis for entrepreneurial growth because it takes the expertise and vision of the entrepreneur and translates it into replicable processes that employees perform to grow the business. Even departments in large organizations could consider themselves to be entrepreneurial entities under the corporate umbrella and reap the same benefits. By definition, a system is replicable, so it's vital to integrate sustainable practices into the system—from concept through development—to ensure sustainable operations.

Systemization can also be driven from the bottom up. I encourage you to study elements of your success to see how they came about and figure out how others can duplicate them—in the spirit of Ray Kroc. He saw how the McDonald brothers operated successful restaurants and, after buying them, systematized their operations so anyone could replicate them.

WHAT NEEDS TO BE SYSTEMATIZED

Business executives are familiar with systemizing large operations of manufacturing products or delivering services. Most are familiar with systemizing the delivery of accounting and management information. But did you know that systemization can be implemented in every nook and cranny—even across the supply chain and product lifecycle?

As an example, consider a less traditional area for systemization: *what you do as a leader*. The percentage of time you spend working *in* your business versus working *on* your business indicates how well you have systematized and delegated your responsibilities.

You know all those magical things only *you* can do? That's your blessing. Unfortunately, that's also your curse. It's a blessing because it has positive impact on your business, but it's a curse because only *you* know how to do it. You can't delegate it to free up your time. Your ego may play a role affirming your expertise—that is, you may believe no one else can do this particular action that's critical to the business. In fact, it's your contribution to the organization.

However, if you could demystify your executive magic by systematizing your core activity and teaching it to others, you'd be even more valuable to your organization. As a result, its operations would be more sustainable. You could free up time to apply your magic to new business issues. Repeatedly doing this leverages your time and talents to their fullest, allowing you to focus in the areas you're most needed. It also leverages your creativity throughout the organization.

You could free up time to apply your magic to new business issues. Repeatedly doing this leverages your time and talents to their fullest, allowing you to focus in the areas you're most needed.

Do you believe that what you do habitually and instinctively *cannot* be systematized? Just about every client I've worked with believes this statement to be true. When you're in the moment of your magic acting instinctively and intuitively, you don't even think about how you're doing it. But when you're put to the test and questioned about it, you can probably transform much of your core activity into defined thought patterns. From that transformative thinking, your system "magically" appears.

Demystifying your magic and *systematizing what you do* allow you to realize your vision as an effective leader. You empower those around you and pass along trust, accountability, and understanding. You also gain time to devote your creative genius to the "entrepreneurial" stage of creating new opportunities and strategies for triple-based profitability. (Review Part Three to see how enhancing your leadership practices can set you on a sustainable course for your business.)

OTHER POTENTIAL AREAS FOR SYSTEMIZATION

Foremost is your sustainable business model. Frequently review your model to create sustainable business practices that can be structured into systems for maximum benefits. The extent to which you need to do this depends on the stage of your business development and, for well-established businesses, how close your existing operations come to your sustainable model.

What else can you systematize? You can examine services that were once outsourced and brought in-house to realize savings, increase control, or improve integration. No doubt what made previous providers successful in delivering these services was systemization. Once in-house, these activities usually start as entrepreneurial "ventures" performed by employees in ways that meet the current need without rigorous company overview, standardization, and integration. The sooner you systematize these functions, the quicker you'll realize advantages from bringing them in-house.

Research and Development (R&D), often overlooked for systemization, mixes art and science to create something new. Structured systems can bring added control yet not stymie creativity. Look at all the "freelance" activities within your R&D organization for their potential to create more sustainable business systems. This might include brainstorming new product ideas and performing research for new market applications. Perhaps not enough ideas are coming forth from the R&D staff for new product ideas. Setting up a system for ideation could make it possible for more employees to participate in the brainstorming effort and generate even more new ideas.

Systemization may also alleviate business constraints. For areas in which your business's potential seems limited, look for production or administrative bottlenecks. Before applying more resources to these problem areas, examine and evaluate the systems involved. What parts of the operation are holding back progress? Often, by systemizing peripheral areas of existing systems, these constraints are reduced or even eliminated. At the same time, see how closely these solutions align with more sustainable approaches. For example, you may have product production delays due to a shortage of a petroleum-based material used in the manufacturing. That might require you to modify the procurement system to handle shortages in a nontraditional way and/or identify materials that could be replaced by more sustainable materials.

HOW TO SYSTEMATIZE

It takes particular skills and tools to determine necessary processes and their logical interrelationships. I favor starting the systemization process with event diagrams; others prefer to use case scenarios. When choosing a tool, matching it with functional support is the most important part. You can find a plethora of system development methodologies, tools, and information for different types of systems available in the marketplace. (These go beyond the scope of this book.)

This list of phases required for developing systems gives you a perspective on the effort involved and the leadership required:

- Forming a stakeholder team
- Assessing the current procedures
- Analyzing business improvements to be realized
- Identifying the changes needed
- Creating a system concept and obtaining stakeholder approval
- Designing a system with all of its operational components
- Getting the design approved by the stakeholder team
- Developing the system
- Documenting system functions
- Testing the system
- Training system users
- Transitioning from the system development to system implementation
- Starting operations

- Monitoring effectiveness in light of the improvements to be realized
- Making necessary adjustments

At this point, your sustainability objectives have already been included in your business improvement strategies targeted to be systematized. Although these phases of system development might seem lengthy or cumbersome, following them will increase your company's efficiency and productivity when setting up any new system.

The level of effort involved is relative to the scope and size of the system. Your role is to provide direction as well as oversee and guide your systems development management team. Overall, you must ensure that the new systems are essential and support your business practices.

HONING SYSTEMS

Before making any system changes, ensure all the components of each change are aligned and fall within business priorities. It requires walking a fine line. Although you want your organization to maintain flexibility for adapting to needed change, you don't want to burden it with the turmoil of excessive change.

Realize that systemization doesn't imply transitioning a business practice into something cast in stone or locking your business into rigid operations. That's why you need to review the systems periodically with an eye to finding better, more sustainable ways to operate.

Don't let your company stagnate with antiquated systems. Inject new energy with changes that support the company's highest priority strategic initiatives as needed. The impact of new technology, feedback from customers, and ideas and suggestions for improvements from employees and other stakeholders require continual

Don't let your company stagnate with antiquated systems. Inject new energy with changes that support the company's highest priority strategic initiatives as needed.

review. This feedback is valuable in assessing the strategic scenarios discussed in Chapter 11.

Want an example? Transitioning McDonald's systems from its inception to supporting today's sustainability directives is an excellent one. It shows how updating systems to support changes in the business direction is valuable while still receiving all the benefits that systemization delivers.

BUILDING IN A MONITORING SYSTEM

Systems need to be monitored to determine their operational performance through select critical success factors (as discussed in Chapter 12). You want to build a means for monitoring those critical success factors into the operational systems.

Some systems measure critical success factors directly as the intended business improvement of the system relates to the critical success factor. Others measure information that will collect into these critical success factors. Make sure you include these informational requirements of the system from inception. Operational trade-offs between accuracy and resources required to provide information (addressed in Chapter 12) should be reviewed in the system development design phase.

If the expense of collecting all relevant data is prohibitive in the initial stages of operation, then make sure the design can adjust for future "plug-in" modules. As the company matures, appending these modules will provide more accurate data without having to develop a whole new system. Like many companies, McDonald's Sweden started with simple steps to reduce overall energy consumption—a measure that's easily reflected in its energy bills. Later, McDonald's enhanced its energy information-gathering systems so it could audit specific equipment to find those needing redesign for greater energy efficiencies. This resulted in new food warmers, fryers, and AVOC systems. In other locations, the timing of their energy consumption helped managers schedule certain tasks for off-peak periods. With this information, they're able to maximize the use of both renewable and non-renewable energy sources.[112]

Systainership™
3.1 Develop Sustainable Systems
1.3
Empowered Employee, Leader & Stakeholder Partnerships
1.1
Mission, Vision, Core Values
2.4
Critical Success Factors
2.3
Aligned Sustainable Strategy
Capital from Business, Owners, and Investors
3.1
Develop Sustainable Systems
Sustainable Systems
Transparent Reporting
1.3
Empowered Employee, Leader & Stakeholder Partnerships
1.1
Mission, Vision, Core Values
Borrowed Resources from the Environment
Sustainable Products/Services from Suppliers
Capital from Business, Owners, and Investors
Community Support
3.2
Accelerate Operational Momentum
Sustainable Products/ Services to the Community
1.3
Empowered Employee, Leader & Stakeholder Partnerships
1.1
Mission, Vision, Core Values
1. & 2.
Transparent Reporting
3.3
Communicate Transparently
Transparent Reporting
Business Results
Profits/ROI to Business, Owners, and Investors
Community Support & Economic Development
Regeneration of Earth's Resources

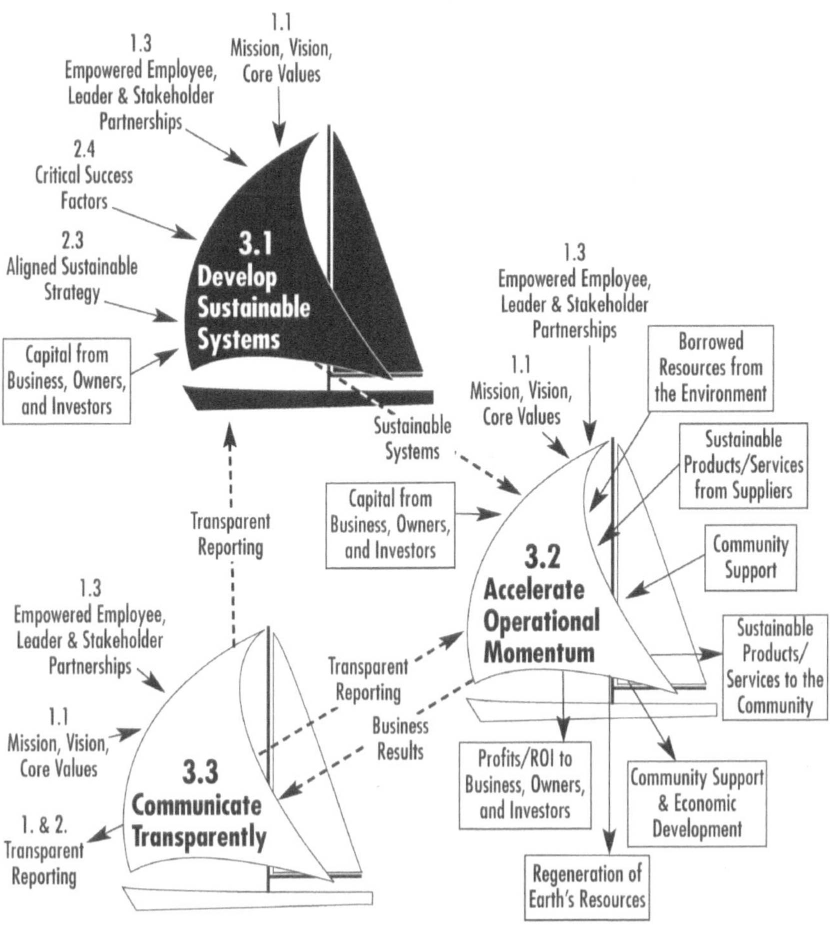

Figure 15

THE SYSTAINERSHIP FUNCTION OF DEVELOPING SUSTAINABLE SYSTEMS

Within Systainership, you can influence the creation of systems that support the growth of triple-based profitability. Systemization provides the means to replicate the success of any business activity. Through the development of sustainable systems, you empower your people to transform approved sustainable strategies into replicable, sustainable business activities. Established critical success factors integrated into systems provide essential monitoring of progress. These systems range from the simple to complex.

You also lead your financial staff in acquiring and allocating capital and other resources required for development and implementation. As leader, you instigate, oversee, and guide your management team to undertake the development of needed systems that are sufficient to support your sustainable business model. When they're complete, you ensure that the systems support the business operations, as illustrated in Figure 15.

You also lead by example in systematizing your leadership blessings. That way, you and other leaders in your company can benefit from passing the torch and applying your essential abilities to new business opportunities.

SUSTAINABILITY BENEFITS THROUGH DEVELOPING SUSTAINABLE SYSTEMS

Systemization within your business provides a mechanism for replicable success in operations, management, and leadership. Continued successes increase the sustainability of your business.

The benefits of systemization are numerous. The systems—

- offer direction, structure, and control.
- unify an organization's activities into a cohesive whole.
- provide a means to align organizational and individual strengths, delegate business activities, and even rotate responsibilities to avoid the pitfalls of stagnation.

- improve efficiency while yielding greater productivity and profitability throughout the organization.

Executing processes through a defined system also increases the stability of your organization. During uncertain times, the systems provide a structure for forward movement. Often this forward movement results in greater clarity to resolve issues. Collectively, these efforts provide greater sustainability.

Developing systems to support your business activity through the lens of sustainability further enhances the sustainability of your business and the world. In fact, some systems are developed specifically to meet your sustainability goals. With sustainable systems in place, your business receives the exponential benefits of both systemization and sustainable business practices. (Refer to Chapter 2 to review the business advantages of sustainability.)

All of this allows your company to realize an increased business value, commanding an increased price tag. Why? Potential buyers perceive they'll have an easier transition to new ownership because the business is defined and operated by a set of systems.

APPLYING SYSTAINERSHIP

Coaching Questions to Move Your Organization Toward Developing Sustainable Systems

1. What activities in your organization are considered "freelance"?
2. What current system would most benefit from a sustainability overhaul to help increase your company's triple-based profitability?
3. What would using a sustainable system to implement one of your organization's new strategic scenarios look like?

For more coaching questions to help your business develop sustainable systems, go to www.SustainableBusinessSystems.com/bq

Call to Action

Pick a key task that you believe only you can do, then turn it into a sustainable system and delegate the activities required to implement it.

Your Insights on Developing Sustainable Systems

____

____

____

____

____

____

Moving Forward with the Systainership Function of Developing Sustainable Systems

What are five steps you can take now to lead your organization toward building sustainable systems? Please list them in order of priority.

1. ____
2. ____
3. ____
4. ____
5. ____

CHAPTER

15

OPTIMIZE MOMENTUM UNDER FULL SAIL

See first that the design is wise and just: that ascertained, pursue it resolutely; do not for one repulse forego the purpose that you resolved to effect.

~ WILLIAM SHAKESPEARE (1564-1616)

Accelerating Global Expansion—A Lesson from Pacific Biodiesel

Robert King questioned what could be done with excessive amounts of used cooking oil being dumped into the landfill on the island of Maui. Reclaiming that oil and refining it into biofuel for the site's diesel generator seemed like a good answer to that question.

That started Pacific Biodiesel, Inc. in 1995, one of the first commercially viable biodiesel producers in the U.S. and owner of the first retail biodiesel pump in America. On Maui, the company diverts more than 80 tons of used cooking oil and 375 tons of grease trap waste *a month* from going into the landfill.[113]

Pacific Biodiesel's core concept is to produce and consume biodiesel locally, thus avoiding the use of vast amounts of energy needed to transport either raw materials or a finished product. This sustainable model for the industry is the epitome of "local" green. Because the supply of used cooking oil is limited, Pacific Biodiesel's technology division efficiently processes mixed multi-feedstock. In fact, in February 2010, it inaugurated the development of its first facility using this technology on the Big Island of Hawaii. It's expected to supply this island with biodiesel plus have enough reserves to increase the supply to neighboring islands currently using their original technology.

The company designs, builds, owns, and operates local processing facilities. Each is scaled to the size of each community it supports to turn multi-feedstock into biodiesel. The use of feedstock for biofuel is controversial because, if done indiscriminately, it can reduce valuable food crops, consume rich agricultural lands that could be used to grow food crops for the world population, or destroy valuable animal habitat. By having individuals locally choose feedstock sources that are right for their community—that is, they're supported by the soil with high yield conversion efficiency, make conservative use of fallow lands, and reduce displacement of food crops and animal habitat—the company minimizes the negative effects of decisions made globally. This demonstrates environmental stewardship while contributing to each community's economy, stability, and safety. With this business model, the company has grown by building additional sites where funding, community, materials, and need align.

In 2007, Pacific Biodiesel spun off its technology division as a separate enterprise called Pacific Biodiesel Technologies. This company now provides expertise, consulting, and management services nationally and internationally. As of 2010, Pacific Biodiesel has continued to evolve its technology and show leadership in the industry. This has been accomplished by providing production efficiencies, versatility, water-free processing, operational experience, high-end fuel quality, multi-feed stock capability, complete recovery of byproducts, and high quality equipment. Its R&D function keeps it on top of the industry game. Its scalable plants produce from .5 to 10 million gallons of biodiesel a year.[114]

As of July 2011, Pacific Biodiesel has completed 12 facilities across the mainland U.S., Hawaii, and Japan with the 13th in construction on the Big Island of Hawaii. The company moves forward in these ways:

- Building new plants community by community
- Expanding existing facilities
- Incorporating their latest technological advances

With determination, its leaders pursue their passion to create the possibility of sustainable diesel fuel for the world. At the same time, they're contributing to the environmental preservation and social backbone of their communities.

---

5 PRINCIPLES FOR CREATING MOMENTUM TO DRIVE SUCCESS

Momentum results from a force or chain of actions that creates forward motion. Having an intentional sustainable direction for your business increases momentum exponentially and leads to reaching your tipping points sooner. Accelerating your momentum in this way helps you achieve your organization's vision with a solid foundation.

Incorporating all the leadership functions discussed to this point will get the ball rolling as you develop your business. Applying these five leadership principles will help you keep the momentum going.

1. *Infuse Inspiration*

   Achieving momentum starts with empowering and motivating yourself, then leading by example. Others will follow your infectious inspiration when you can express what "lights you up." Helping others in your organization see a world of possibility is needed especially during times of structure changes and downsizing.

   How do you infuse inspiration into any organizational change?

   - Tell success stories about the company and other partner organizations.
   - Use examples of everyday heroes to inspire others to see the world of possibilities.

- Let your employees ask "what if?" questions.
- Use humor to bring people together.
- Project yourself as a contributor who's making a difference for the company, even if you're not sure how to do this.
- Encourage others to stand for what they believe is important to the business.

Whatever you do, follow through with a burst of activity to capitalize on the inspiration and motivation out of the gate.

2. *Relate to Purpose*

It's important to show how the changes contribute to the higher vision, goals, and sustainability of your organization. That requires you to communicate to your implementation teams the purpose of any new system and the adjustments you want them to make.

Often, changes are delegated down a chain of command in a way that loses all connection to their intended purpose. They're seen as just another endeavor to put money in the pockets of the owners at others' expense. When stakeholders see this as "change for the sake of change," there's no buy-in.

Putting change into the context of the new strategies and systems being implemented makes the company vision relevant to everyone involved—from management to operations. Rolling project benefits up to the level of the corporate vision sparks motivation and conveys a greater understanding of the purpose. Leaders who can clearly communicate objectives and responsibilities to others avoid ambiguities. For Pacific Biodiesel, each new plant brings the world closer to realizing a sustainable diesel fuel supply for world communities. People get inspired when the purpose comes from the core of the company; it also empowers team members in making decisions.

Remember, employees want to see how their lives and work will be advanced by the change. They want to feel vested in any new strategy and its results. They want to feel part of the effort and have a fulfilling role, not only with the company as a whole, but in employing their individual potential in the new projects and procedures. This is reinforced when critical success factors used to evaluate individual and team performance connect to the organization's critical success factors that are communicated openly.

3. *Shine a Light on the Possibilities*

   A most demanding task for leaders is to radiate the realm of possibility when everything around seems to be whirling off course. Leaders must confidently stand in their vision, living and expressing it in every conversation, no matter how difficult the challenges, obstacles, needs of short-term goals, or accumulated fears of employees.

   Radiating the realm of possibilities annuls the assumptions of doom and gloom that can permeate and undermine any goals not achieved. Aren't these but merely a missed waypoint along your course? Your destination—the overarching vision of your business—has not changed! Your employees are still on board. So seek to rededicate their commitment and revitalize their energy through these challenges.

   To accomplish this, you may need to continually reframe difficulties perceived into new possibilities. Lead by example with this new view of the business, embracing it in all you do and say. Also, bring attention to efforts that are on-course with what's possible under the guiding vision as well as those that are not. Efforts that are off-course may be temporarily lacking connection to the vision.

   To re-generate possibilities in those areas, what could you do?

   - Become the corporate channel for heralding the organization's vision.
   - Create inspiration through audio and visual reminders using company blogs, posters, announcements, and so on.
   - Turn the effort into a business game, bringing an element of fun into the mix while creating a new and different energy.
   - Point out the hidden connections that connect everyone's efforts to each other.

- In the face of fear, turn employees toward their passions and compassion for each other, expressing emotionally *what* they do and *why* they do it.
- Create tolerance for the creative tension and possibility for the synchronicity of missing pieces of the puzzle to appear.
- Be courageous by "being" your vision.
- Remind people to continue their sail across the sea of sustainability, not conquer every "green sea monster" in the world.

All these efforts promote a positive mindset and keep projects moving in a productive direction. With your help, everyone in your organization will support what's important going forward and keep the possibilities alive.

4. Promote Persistence

Because momentum happens through time and effort, your company must persistently take action, step after step, even in the face of poor results. As Thomas Edison is quoted as saying, "I have not failed; I've just found 10,000 ways that won't work." Although this number is likely exaggerated, Edison's toughest invention—the incandescent electric light bulb for the consumer market—required making countless attempts before he discovered a workable solution. What if he had stopped and never reached his goal?

Edison and others show how such ventures are undertakings of continual learning that embrace both success and failure. Mistakes happen; risks taken don't always work out. To learn from all of your efforts, though, be sure to foster an environment that tolerates mistakes and encourages, not discourages, new ideas.

Persistence requires getting beyond the pitfalls, the barriers, and the disappointments. Leadership by example plays a key role, and your attitude is absolutely influential. When taking action gets tough, break it down into small, manageable pieces to keep moving. Encourage everyone to do five things, large or small, each day to advance the goal. When necessary, create support teams to keep the attention on the *intention* of the changes being undertaken. Look for support to come from any number of directions: logistic, technical, management, executive coaching, etc. Understand how and why the effort is being sidelined to determine the appropriate assistance.

For Pacific Biodiesel, its first plant was up and running in 1996 with two more plants installed and operational by 2002. By late 2010, 12 plants were in operation and another in development. See what momentum its leaders built?

Success contagiously excites people, boosts their morale, and gives new energy. So build on the success of one model to create the next. Have courage to try new approaches. Success increases your ability to calculate risk. When you experience repeated success, you reach a tipping point that propels this momentum into a whole new realm.

But what if the tide turns against the positive momentum you want? While pursuing a sustainable strategy, new circumstances could affect your progress. You have to incorporate this feedback into the leadership function of alignment (discussed in Chapter 10). All the while, make sure any strategic alterations to keep up the momentum hold true to your company's mission.

5. *Champion Achievement*

Success begets success. That's why Pacific Biodiesel celebrates each new plant start-up.

A high level of motivation propels you into the next action that quickly becomes another success. To ensure continued momentum, make time for celebrating your successes. But schedule celebrations accordingly. A break in the flow of action at the wrong time can turn the tables and decrease motivation.

Systainership™

3.2 Accelerate Operational Momentum

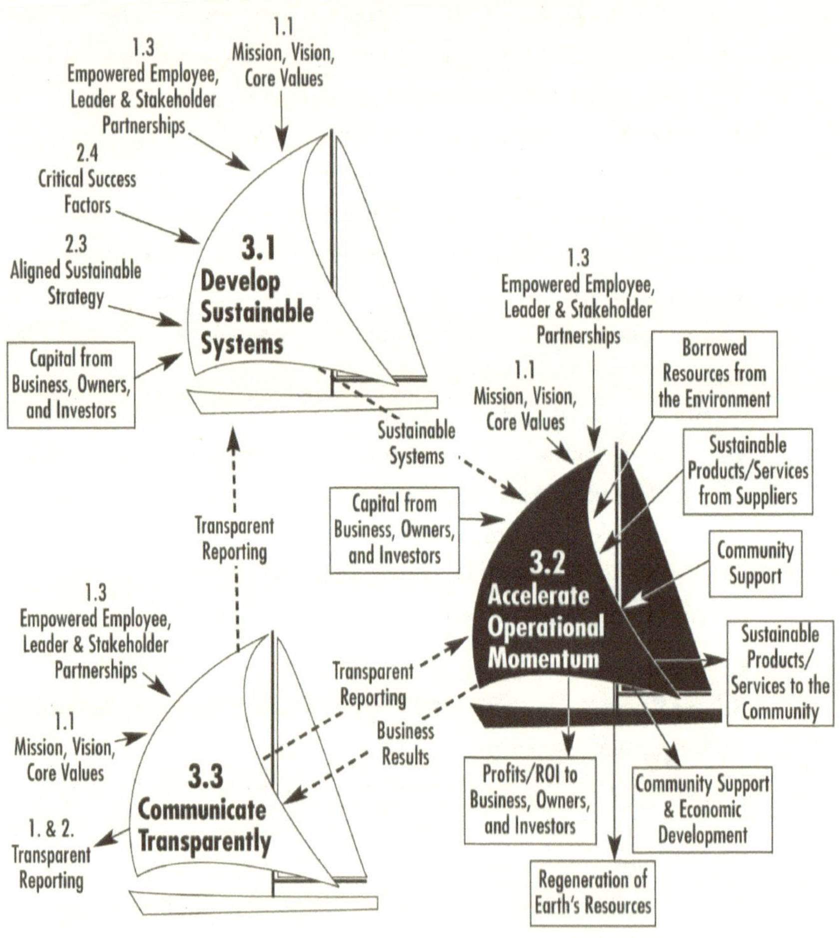

Figure 16

Yet, for leaders to recognize achievement, it doesn't take much time or break the flow and it boosts the achiever's morale and sense of fulfillment.

As part of the natural pause in the momentum, always celebrate and reward people when large projects end and when major goals are reached. Celebratory events can even start a new wave of momentum to spearhead the next movement forward.

THE SYSTAINERSHIP FUNCTION OF ACCELERATING OPERATIONAL MOMENTUM

Accelerating operational momentum in Systainership uses the new sustainable strategies and supporting systems developed to move the operations of a company toward its desired outcomes. This leadership function supports the operations while propelling the company forward. The critical success factors, integral to the systems, assess how this movement is advancing toward the goals set. See Figure 16.

As a leader, your role is to inspire a strong sense of purpose and possibility to propel movement. You need persistence to hurdle the obstacles. You want to promote achievement in a way that supports the company's momentum. All this leads to the tipping point of success.

This comes together as the rewards of triple-based profitability. That's when sustainable products and services are being produced at an acceptable rate of return for investors. At the same time, they're tapping into resources in a regenerative way and supporting the community socially, economically, and culturally.

SUSTAINABILITY BENEFITS THROUGH ACCELERATING OPERATIONAL MOMENTUM

Momentum is a leader's best friend. In the physical sense, it's measured by the time it takes to bring a moving mass to rest when under a constant opposing force. So, for any business, the greater the positive momentum, the healthier, more sustainable the business will be. It will have greater fortitude to withstand the tests of time.

In pursuing direct sustainability strategies, momentum helps you—

- realize benefits for both your company and the world.
- achieve your goals faster and reap the benefits sooner.
- have the power to conquer the obstacles along the way more easily.
- move past mistakes quickly and power through change.
- increase motivation, which leads to greater achievement.
- get everyone in the organization enthused to work toward priority goals and make the changes needed.

APPLYING SYSTAINERSHIP

Coaching Questions to Move Your Organization Toward Accelerating Operational Momentum

1. How much time do you think you should devote to creating momentum for change within your organization?
2. What new strategies are you launching that need your attention so they can create momentum that will improve the chances for greater sustainability of your business?
3. Where is there negative momentum within your organization that needs to be turned around?

For more coaching questions to help your business accelerate operational momentum, go to www.SustainableBusinessSystems.com/bq

Call to Action

Pick an area within your organization where progress seems stagnant and create a succession of successes to build momentum.

Your Insights on Accelerating Operational Momentum

____

____

____

____

____

____

Moving Forward with the Systainership Function of Accelerating Operational Momentum

What are five steps you can take now to lead your organization toward accelerating operational momentum? Please list them in order of priority.

1. ____
2. ____
3. ____
4. ____
5. ____

CHAPTER

16

COMMUNICATING PROGRESS "MADE GOOD"

You are the lens in the beam. You can only receive, give, and possess the light as the lens does. If you seek yourself, you rob the lens of its transparency. You will know life and be acknowledged by it according to your degree of transparency, your capacity, that is, to vanish as an end, and remain purely as a means.

~ DAG HAMMARSKJOLD (1905-1961)

Open, Honest, and Accountable— A Lesson from Timberland Company

The Timberland Company equips people to work, live, and play in their environment—country, city, mountain or sea—by manufacturing comfortable footwear, clothes, and gear that withstands the elements. Its mission? "To equip people to make a difference in their world. We do this by making outstanding products and by trying to make a difference in the communities where we live and work." Timberland considers everyone—its employees, retailers, manufacturers, the communities in which they live and operate, its customers, suppliers, and all other stakeholders—one diverse team working together to make a difference. Its core values are simple and direct: humanity, humility, integrity, and excellence. (The facts about Timberland presented here come from the company's website.[115])

This publicly traded company answers to a diverse group. Its leaders encourage all stakeholders to get engaged. They welcome ideas, feedback, challenge, and innovation through inspired conversation and collaboration—all based on a solid foundation of transparency and accountability.

All company reports are available to stakeholders and the public on its website. That includes its latest financial reports, corporate responsibility report, stock price, sustainability index dashboard, strategy, and partner collaborations. The site even provides the frequency of the reports and what's available as interim information between the publication of full reports. The online product catalog uses icons to relate product sustainability information. And although Timberland provides enough information to fill a book, it doesn't *read* like a book because it's "packaged" with targeted sections.

Doing business with its partners, Timberland collaborates in each of the its four pillar areas of business: product, environment, community, and social justice. Its leaders encourage collaboration with anyone who wants to participate through the company's online forum, Timberland Earthkeepers. Here, any stakeholder can read blog articles, make comments, ask challenging questions, review quarterly metrics, and more.

Timberland leaders happily report company successes, but they don't hold back when talking about their challenges and how they're addressing them. For example, they used to do periodic audits of their international manufacturing facilities to improve conditions for workers. Over time, the progress made seemed to backslide and didn't seem sustainable. Timberland then changed its approach from *monitoring* to *consulting*. This change gets at the root cause of issues and results in partnering with the company and other organizations to make improvements.

With its focus of building a community of trust, Timberland has achieved positive results as its employees continue to operate with the company values in mind, and with openness and honesty. The result? Beneficial partnerships at all levels of the business.

Is Timberland achieving sustainability perfectly? No, no company is, but its transparency earns high marks! Looking at its reports and reading about its business focus provides key information for people to easily see where this company is heading. Timberland has proven that being transparent and accountable is good business.

TRANSPARENCY IN REPORTING

Transparent reporting has become a hot topic these days. Advancing from Web to Web-2 to Web-3 technologies, the availability of information is reaching mind-boggling proportions. Having open channels of communication has become more important than ever.

Large corporations are required to produce financial documents reflecting effective governance, investment decision making, and regulatory compliance. This information builds credibility and confidence among external stakeholders of the organization.

A triple-based business foundation calls for two new levels of transparent reporting. One level is environmental impact—the effect its operations, products, packaging, and distribution are having on the environment. The second is human impact—how the communities where it operates are affected.

These two new reporting areas have become consumer-driven and activist-driven. Impact issues measure high on the list of priority concerns for growing numbers of customers and NGOs. Companies making inroads in these areas have created brand confidence and credibility as they develop stronger loyalties among all their stakeholders.

Transparent company reporting enables leaders to identify opportunities for flow of capital to improve growth and value at a reduced risk. But how deep within the company should it be extended? And how does it affect privately held companies?

I had the opportunity to coach members of a leadership team from a privately held corporation. They were struggling with communication and support issues. One of their needs was getting access to closely held financial reporting. They believed they couldn't make the best decisions without that access. Lacking this information, they found themselves making all kinds of assumptions, and from there, second-guessing themselves. They also deemed many corporate directives unrealistic, which led to feelings of resentment that had been building for years.

Transparent company reporting enables leaders to identify opportunities for flow of capital to improve growth and value at a reduced risk.

Overall, they saw themselves as part of a dedicated team that's frustrated by working toward unachievable goals. Their feelings of dissatisfaction and resentment lessened their motivation and credibility within their own divisions of the company.

In the absence of the truth, there's no limit to where our imagination takes us. Story making is part of human nature unless we are highly trained in personal development to recognize this and stop to search for the truth. Even if we have this insight, without necessary information, we are left to rely on trust. But how trusting can one be of another who doesn't trust you with the information you deem necessary? And if the top managers feel apprehensive, can we build trust from the bottom up through the employees?

What if such a leadership team chose to be totally transparent and conveyed the information they needed to the company's CEO? What if they also cited how this lack of information affects them and the whole organization? What if each of these leaders became totally transparent in reporting to their own divisions through formal reports, meetings, and daily communications?

I hit this challenge head on when crafting my summary coaching report for this company. Each participant completed an assessment form at the close of the consulting session. The results they noted were very good, but not as exemplary as I anticipated. Why didn't the results meet my expectations? I could have just omitted this from my summary report; it wasn't a piece my client had requested. However, this team had declared a need for transparent reporting from company leaders. I believed *down to my core* it was necessary for me to take the high road and be totally transparent with my findings. So rather than feeling apprehensive, I realized by providing the whole truth, everyone would benefit. It led to being in total agreement on how to reorganize the participants for future sessions. It also created a synergy to produce far better results in our fresh efforts ahead.

Because transparent reporting is beneficial at all levels, I encourage you to disseminate information more transparently than ever within your organization.

GOING BEYOND COMPLIANCE

From Timberland's example and my own, transparent reporting goes far beyond government and regulatory compliance. And it goes beyond disseminating management reporting down the hierarchy on a perceived "need to know" basis.

> *When stakeholders know the whole situation, they can better align themselves with your efforts and make informed decisions.*

Transparent reporting lays out exactly what your company's doing, how you're doing it, and how well you're doing it. When stakeholders know the whole situation, they can better align themselves with your efforts and make informed decisions. When they sense honesty from you, trust and loyalty follow.

RELEASING THE FEAR

Many executives fear releasing company information so they hold what's beyond compliance close to the vest. This fear stems from—

- having "private" business made public.
- the possibility of receiving negative criticism. (Are the executives doing enough?)
- potentially releasing trade secrets. (Will the company lose its competitive edge?)
- possible failure degrading their public image. (Will the company's reputation get a black eye?)

But fear-based decision making can hold back both the leaders and their companies. Feelings of insecurity put out vibrations felt throughout the organization and beyond, creating an atmosphere of doubt and conjecture. The appearance that something is being hidden causes speculation. What does management not want us to know? Who's benefiting at our expense? Rumors run rampant. Relationships are perceived as "you win/I lose," which affects loyalty and diminishes productivity.

What's needed? A mindset shift by your leadership team to turn the fears of transparent reporting into beneficial business opportunities.

How could you turn the fear of judgment into opportunities for honesty, humility, and learning? Or turn the fear of disclosing valuable information to competitors into a chance to set your company apart and even reduce competition? Some fears could be turned into opportunities such as partnering with industry leaders to jointly move your industry forward.

This goes back to considering failures to be valuable sources of information on how not to proceed on your journey—just as Timberland did when trying to improve working conditions in its foreign manufacturing facilities. Instead, look for opportunities to commit to a new direction. And what's good about giving out "private" business information? It leads to trust, better decision making, and employee enrollment. I agree that certain information needs to remain private, especially at the employee level, but at nowhere near the volume of information businesses tend to protect.

7 GUIDELINES FOR EFFECTIVE TRANSPARENT COMMUNICATION

Consider these seven guidelines for disclosing the correct information in proven ways.

1. *Acknowledge Your Responsibility*

   Is it the destiny of business to be responsible to its owners by generating a good return on the money invested in the business, private or public, and being responsible for its long-term viability as well as the world in which it operates? The answer from many stakeholders is a resounding YES.

   Providing information on the role your company assumes in this broad responsibility is a first step in transparent reporting. Some leaders convey this through their company's mission, vision, and/or values. Others see their role as being supportive to their overriding mission, and they report on it separately.

   Just know that, in some way, stakeholders want to know the heart and soul of your business. They expect your company to provide that information because it demonstrates the ethics by which business is conducted to achieve economic, social, and environmental stewardship.

2. *Gather Relevant Information*

   Establishing the correct critical success factors (discussed in Chapter 12) measure your progress on the path to your business success. Again, the level of information needs to be gauged to its audience in order to convey understanding without overwhelm. It should also address what stakeholders want to know, backed by levels of information they trust, in a context that allows them to evaluate progress.

   The product icons on Timberland's website provide a good example. Each product tag has specific icons pertaining to how that product was created. If customers want more information, such as manufacturing standards and descriptions of the ethics of the company which these icons represent, they can read the CSR report. Once customers retrieve the level of information they desire, they can rely on the icons to represent the details of what they have learned. The icons then serve as relevant, sufficient information to help curious customers make purchasing decisions.

Environmental NGOs are interested in the company's environmental footprint, how its represented, and what information backs it up. Once satisfied, they can then use one or more of the company's dashboard measures to follow their progress.

To clarify, the term "relevant" doesn't include your company's trade secrets. With transparent reporting, companies report on the performance of products and services already released into the market. They aren't releasing information on new business developments not yet protected by patents or other legal means.

On the other hand, companies looking for collaborative development of new products within an industry actually do release early development plans. Open source software developments such as Google Wave and the website content management systems Joomla and Drupal are such examples. Within your company, you'll develop the framework for releasing information that's appropriate for your company's path to success.

3. *Convey Appropriate Messaging*

Dashboard reports such as Timberland's help you view the company's status at a glance and can help you conceptualize streams of raw data for focus and understanding. But is this appropriate messaging?

Conveying any company's information provides an opportunity to engage another entity into a positive relationship with the company. This message can potentially "market" your organization not only to customers but to suppliers, NGOs, stockholders, and so on. The information should be conveyed like any marketing message is delivered to customers—with impact, effectiveness, consistency of brand, trust, and honesty. It should communicate benefits, identify with them, speak their language, and answer their questions before they're asked.

This seems difficult when preparing "one message for all" as companies do by putting their information on the internet. However, consider that *all* your messages have to be consistent to be credible. The level of detail varies on who your audience is, but it's still important that the message consistently rolls up to your key points. As relationships develop over time, stakeholders go to the information they deem most informative for their purposes. For those following Timberland's dashboard over time, it stands alone as the most sufficient, succinct, relevant information they want and can trust.

Internal company messaging is analogous with the same rollup of supporting data but requires more detail than the collective information put out to public stakeholders. The critical success factors are separated into supporting components, down to individual contribution levels within the organization. These become the motivational performance indicators that are reviewed to assess how to improve results at the detailed operational levels.

Transparent reporting includes business regulatory compliance. When your company is working to comply with agency standards of operation, reporting that progress could improve your company's credibility with stakeholders.

4. *Share Best Practices*

Sharing industry best practices also conveys what you're doing and how you're doing it. Helping create industry standards appeals to other companies following in your footsteps and might also appeal to industry peers when comparing the relative success of various approaches. Their best practices will interest you in the same way.

Any best practice that is a technological innovation unique to your company would be handled in the same as any other technological advance, perhaps with an application for patent and corresponding press releases.

5. *Tailor Your Message for the Sake of Comparison*

If the information being released about your company—its

products or services and the triple-based foundation on which they're developed and delivered—is a competitive edge for your company, then your message might need tailoring. Sometimes a transparent message needs to be reformatted for comparison to competitor's parameters. Pacific Biodiesel does this nicely on its website. There, it contrasts plant facilities and operations of other plant developers in an interesting narrative format.[116]

6. *Eliminate Green-washing*

Green-washing means releasing information about your product, service, or company that leads others to believe it might be "greener" than it is.

Some companies make generalized claims of being green or selling green products without providing information on the sustainability efforts of the company and areas for improvement. This can start quite innocently in obtaining a green *label* of some kind, but then not following up with company intentions and stakeholder information needs. Some companies stop after making early accomplishments and claims, with the intention of gaining market advantages from it. That's how green-washing creates distrust and confusion among stakeholders.

As mentioned in Chapter 12, the proliferation of green recognitions and certifications by various NGOs has contributed to this consumer distrust, but certifications are losing their significance. Their intent was to make it easier for consumers to recognize green products, but today, consumers are more confused than ever.

These third-party certifications do not convey information necessary for—

- determining improved performance either at the managerial level or at the productivity level.
- consumer comparisons.
- vendor requirements.
- employee contribution.
- stockholders evaluations of triple-based profitability.
- support from your SEC team or mastermind group.

Instead of green-washing, move your company forward with the information necessary for all stakeholders to measure the progress you're making.

Attaining certifications—for example, an organic certification for agriculture—might be standard in your industry. Providing your own transparent reporting along with that will back up the certification and provide trust in the recognition. Stakeholders will see exactly where your company is on its journey and be able to align with it. This will give them a reason to engage with your company over others with the same certification.

7. *Solicit Feedback*

Soliciting feedback from stakeholders shows your genuine interest in improving your message and your journey. It demonstrates how humble your organization is and how much it values working partnerships. Your willingness to invite others into your community—to let them become part of your journey—upholds the principle of inclusivity and expands your partnerships in ways you hadn't conceived.

Getting feedback provides another mechanism for growth, so invite and welcome it from both inside and outside of the company. Your frontline employees know the operation from within. Your external stakeholders have their own unique and valuable perspective. Find a way to make feedback a two-way street open to learning sessions in which challenges are addressed and solutions discussed. Doing this reinforces the working relationships and helps make partners (including your own employees) more self-sufficient in finding new solutions.

THE SYSTAINERSHIP FUNCTION OF COMMUNICATING TRANSPARENTLY

In the function of communicating transparently, you orchestrate the flow of information about your business with your systems constantly providing updates on all critical success factors. You guide the selection

Systainership™
3.3 Communicate Transparently
1.1
Mission, Vision,
Core Values
1.3
Empowered Employee,
Leader & Stakeholder
Partnerships
2.4
Critical Success
Factors
2.3
Aligned Sustainable
Strategy
Capital from
Business, Owners,
and Investors
3.1
Develop
Sustainable
Systems
1.3
Empowered Employee,
Leader & Stakeholder
Partnerships
1.1
Mission, Vision,
Core Values
Borrowed
Resources from
the Environment
Sustainable
Products/Services
from Suppliers
Sustainable
Systems
Capital from
Business, Owners,
and Investors
Transparent
Reporting
Community
Support
3.2
Accelerate
Operational
Momentum
Sustainable
Products/
Services to the
Community
1.3
Empowered Employee,
Leader & Stakeholder
Partnerships
1.1
Mission, Vision,
Core Values
Transparent
Reporting
Business
Results
3.3
Communicate
Transparently
1. & 2.
Transparent
Reporting
Profits/ROI to
Business, Owners,
and Investors
Community Support
& Economic
Development
Regeneration of
Earth's Resources

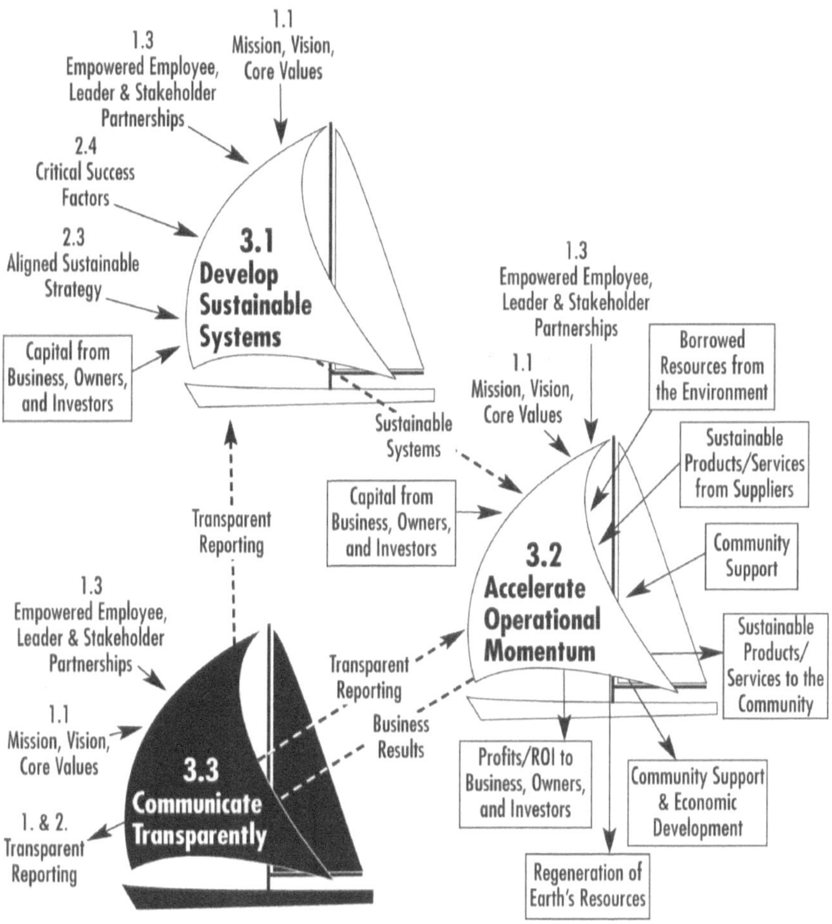

Figure 17

and frequencies of reporting, packaging them into meaningful, relevant, and appropriate messages for all stakeholders. Even when report models are used—for example, GRI, Balanced Scorecard, or ISO 14000—the information content can still follow your established guidelines for transparency. Smaller companies scale the types of information to meet their own needs, using the guidelines to create their own reporting formats. You lead the way in this function, inviting and providing feedback, creating learning opportunities, and developing powerful partnerships with all stakeholders. See Figure 17.

As information is fed back into this leadership system, it closes the loop of the system for the next round of business growth on your sustainable journey. The Systainership Program has its own special dashboard reporting feature to facilitate this.[117]

SUSTAINABILITY BENEFITS THROUGH COMMUNICATING TRANSPARENTLY

Leading your organization to communicate transparently is like having an open book on the efforts your organization has undertaken to become more sustainable. It sheds light on just where your company is on its journey. It's designed to address the information needs of all stakeholders and communicate the critical success factors of the organization in a meaningful way.

Communicating transparently provides significant benefits on the journey to creating a sustainable enterprise. In particular, it—

- creates accountability leading to credibility.
- generates consumer trust and loyalty that sustains a company through the tides of economic change.
- provides necessary information to align purpose and values to create motivation, synergy, and cooperation among all stakeholders.
- internally markets strategies to all levels of the organization, transforming strategies into clear actions and systems.
- aligns everyone within the organization so they're all striving to meet your triple-based profitability.

All this leads to greater effectiveness, efficiency, and productivity—and ultimately sustainability and profitability.

Because transparency is humbling, it makes your organization appear genuine, sincere, and approachable. As a result, your partnerships will be deeper, stronger, and more accepting than ever before.

APPLYING SYSTAINERSHIP

Coaching Questions to Move Your Organization Toward Communicating Transparently

1. Which of your bottom lines is suffering the most from lack of transparency?
2. What new business possibilities could arise from making the information from question #1 more transparent?
3. How could you appropriately message that information to create new business possibilities and greater accountability?

For more coaching questions to help your business business communicate transparently, go to www.SustainableBusinessSystems.com/bq

Call to Action

Pick a stakeholder with whom you would like to collaborate. Invite that person to work with you in developing information needed to create a cohesive, synergistic relationship.

Your Insights on Communicating Transparently

____

____

____

____

____

____

Moving Forward with the Systainership Function of Communicating Transparently

What are five steps you can take now to lead your organization toward communicating transparently? Please list them in order of priority.

1. ____
2. ____
3. ____
4. ____
5. ____

PART FIVE

Results! Your Business Approaches 100% Sustainability

I am always doing that which I cannot do, in order that I may learn how to do it.

~ PABLO PICASSO (1881-1973)

CHAPTER

17

BRING YOUR DREAM BACK INTO YOUR BUSINESS

Change will not come if we wait for some
other person or some other time.
We are the ones we've been waiting for.
We are the change that we seek.

~ BARACK OBAMA (1961-)

AGE OF CONNECTEDNESS

Business has evolved from the days of bartering (driven by necessity) through business models such as capitalism (driven by money) and now sustainability (driven by social awakening). Each business generation builds on what has previously evolved. Business is now driven by necessity, money, and social awakening. Many lines drawn between the methodologies and disciplines have been erased, and leaders of organizations look at business solutions in an ever-increasingly comprehensive and systemic way.

In this Age of Connectedness, society has become more integrated than in previous eras. Individuals are involved in their local communities *and* participate in communities worldwide through the advances of the internet. With their instant consumer ratings, social networks affect how we do business. We have expanded human health and well-being to include the holistic wellness of the mind, body, and spirit. People in developed countries are experiencing greater fulfillment by being able to combine financial goals with a purpose in life. Science and theology are merging in many cosmological studies. Historical separations of vocational disciplines are being erased, creating openings to comprehensive ideas, challenges, and solutions. Universities are expanding degree programs that combine multiple educational disciplines.

In the same way, the historical lines separating profitability and world stewardship are also being erased. Examples throughout this book have shown that strategies good for the world and also good for businesses' bottom lines are improving. Businesses are touching on spirituality by aligning their mission and vision with core values that resonate in the hearts of the employees and customers they attract.

In greater numbers than ever, artistic right-brained people are working side by side with logical left-brained developers to design products that go beyond functionality. Together, they're testing new ways to integrate the complex needs of their consumers. In addition, companies are partnering with other businesses, NGOs, and governments on programs that provide economic, social, and environmental benefits all around.

Perhaps we can conclude that business is unifying with the world. And *that* is good business!

SHOOT FOR THE STARS TO REACH THE MOON

Is 100% sustainability achievable for either your business or the world? Maybe, or maybe not. But certainly *not* if we never strive for it.

By striving for sustainability, businesses are able to—

- create a collective energy that they move forward.
- make progress on multiple fronts.
- create immeasurably more meaningful connections.
- move toward the legacies leaders want for their businesses.

A fully sustainable world requires solutions that aren't yet conceivable—and perhaps won't be for generations to come. However, sailing this course puts next-generation leaders further ahead. These future leaders will benefit from our advances today just as the following generations will benefit from their innovations. Sustainability will define the next evolution of doing business.

Are you up for it?

Focused and On Course—A Lesson from Sea Sweetleeder

Remember our character, Sea Sweetleeder, and the challenges his company faced in Chapter 1? Let's continue his story.

Sea is committed to creating a sustainable corporate culture. In building this foundation, he has—

- aligned with celebrity yo-yo sports heroes who also want to foster a more sustainable world.
- engaged his product development team to brainstorm sustainable product life cycles for products that will also serve the up-and-coming generation of yo-yo sport enthusiasts.
- conducted a company-wide campaign to roll out a new shared vision, mission, and values initiative.
- emphasized partnering with employees, suppliers, and the communities in which they operate.
- improved employee loyalty by including workers in improving how the business runs and letting them volunteer for sustainability projects.
- had employees set up an online customer community to share event postings, tips, and techniques from yo-yo experts and yo-yo fundraising activities.

In addition, Sea has gained control of his day by systematizing tasks and training his next-in-command to do them for him. Other leaders in the company are exploring options for more sustainable manufacturing strategies than those currently outsourced to China. They believe their new product development efforts will lead them in the right direction.

In the meantime, Nieu-Mart has recognized Sea's company

as its most forward-thinking supplier for the sport of yo-yo.

Together, their leaders are exploring sustainable ways of distributing their products.

Amazing results keep showing up! After hearing about the new direction the company has adopted, the former VP of manufacturing asked to come back.

Although Sea can't say all the problems are solved, his people clearly enjoy a new energy, focus, and spirit to address their challenges. They believe long-term strategies will help them come up with even better solutions to their short-term problems. Next year, they'll create their first corporate social responsibility report and share their accomplishments with others. On this journey that embraces environmental stewardship, community support, and responsible development and profitability, Sea wants everyone traveling with his company to enjoy the ride.

Sea himself is experiencing an excitement he hasn't felt since he launched his company 14 years ago. Why? Because he's finally building it into the dream business he'd always wanted—with

SYSTAINERSHIP IN BRIEF:

1. Build a Sustainable Culture
   - 1.1 Impart Stability
   - 1.2 Strengthen Flexibility
   - 1.3 Empower People
2. Set a Sustainable Course
   - 2.1 Create Focus
   - 2.2 Invent Strategic Scenarios
   - 2.3 Assess Sustainability Alignment
   - 2.4. Establish Critical Success Factors
3. Generate Sustainable Momentum
   - 3.1 Develop Sustainable Systems
   - 3.2 Accelerate Operational Momentum
   - 3.3 Communicate Transparently

more potential than he'd ever conceived. And he's not doing it alone. Once again, he's captaining his ship and loving it.

WHERE ARE YOU NOW?

If you've read this far, it means you're ready to lead your team into dreaming big for your business. Let sustainability pull you into its existence rather than pushing it into yours.

> *Let sustainability pull you into its existence rather than pushing it into yours.*

Doing that requires a shift of mindset—to honor the *possibility* of this sustainable world *and* your sustainable business with passionate intent. It requires converting "overwhelm" into "focus" that facilitates a fast track to your sustainable business model.

It's one thing to read this book and get ideas about a sustainability leadership system to move your company forward. But it's only in *applying* this sustainability system that you'll realize the full engagement of your employees. In fact, you'll achieve even greater rewards when they co-create sustainable business practices under your leadership. This type of committed activity sets up opportunities for learning that will lead to your company's sustainability breakthroughs and long-term profitability. Look for sustainable development to provide immediate fulfillment—a powerful key to success that isn't possible any other way.

It's time to lead your team into dreaming *BIG* for your business.

AFTERWORD

Wherever you see a successful business,
someone once made a courageous decision.

~ PETER DRUCKER (1909-2005)

A fire burns within to build your enterprise. You perceive an energetic new approach to leadership that gets you to set sails with confidence. You want your business to become sustainably profitable as you create the business legacy of your dreams.

Where do you go from here?

First, pull yourself out of day-to-day business activities and look at your company through your new sustainability leadership lens. Schedule time to use the tools at the end of each chapter and do this systemically.

If you haven't already done so, go back and confidently step into every question in each chapter with your business in mind. Roll the questions around a bit and then record your answers. As you do, you'll see gaps between *where your business is now* and *where you want it to be.* These gaps help you determine your next actions as you lead your company toward a vision of greater sustainability. Specifically, these gaps will help you define any missing direction, foundation, strategies, and supporting systems in your business.

This book has introduced you to the fundamentals of Systainership, the first component of the complete Systainership Program, which includes these benefits:

- Understand the principles and relationships of the sustainability leadership functions presented in Systainership and work with the tools provided.
- Participate in the Systainership Officers' Club for leadership support through executive matching. As a result, you'll form a cohesive, supportive mastermind group facilitated in virtual meetings. Your goal? To leverage shared expertise in a highly

focused manner. The Systainership Log, a sustainability dashboard reporting system helps you set and track your critical success factors as you sail through the process.

- Gain personal support to implement this program through Systainership Fast-Track Executive Coaching. This one-to-one coaching accelerates your progress to triple-based profitability.

You can learn details and complete benefits of The Systainership Program at www.SustainableBusinessSystems.com. Remember, The Systainership Program supports involved leaders to discover their businesses' gaps and bridge them productively, sustainably, and profitably.

The Systainership leadership principles and functional relationships will guide your journey. Although they provide an excellent start, don't hesitate to get support. To learn how the complete program can help you with your business, I suggest you fill out the form in the back of this book and send it to the address there. Or you could fill it out online at www.SustainableBusinessSystems.com/Services/Systainership.

While differentiating your business from others in an expansive marketplace, this Systainership Program will take your business to new destinations. And the bonus? You and your employees will feel passion for your business like you've never experienced before.

Build the principles of Systainership into your leadership and sail your company smoothly into a sustainable world. Remember:

The sea of wisdom washes in, waiting for us to have the courage to ride its waves.

Shall we start?

~ LYNN VANLEEUWEN, SUSTAINABLE BUSINESS SYSTEMS

ENDNOTES

1 United Nations General Assembly, *Report on the World Commission on Environment and Development*, December 1987, http://www.un.org/documents/ga/res/42/ares42-187.htm (Accessed October 2010).

2 Agilent Technologies, Awards, http://jobs.agilent.com/who_we_are/awards.html (May 1, 2010).

3 *ADP Brings Enhanced Onboarding to Agilent*, LRP Publications, Human Resource Executive Online, http://www.hrexecutive.com/HRE/story.jsp?storyId=142326512 (Nov. 1, 2008).

4 Derek Monell, *Kaiser Permanente's Pioneering E-Medicine is Green*, Kona-Kohala Chamber of Commerce Kuleana Workshop, (Kailua-Kona, HI), March 10, 2010.

5 Randi Kahn, *Kaiser Permanente Honored as Leader in Health Information Technology*, http://xnet.kp.org/newscenter/pressreleases/nat/2009/040609himssstage7.html (Accessed April 6, 2009).

6 Luanne Bradley, *Save Trees and Thrive*, Ecosalon, http://www.ecosalon.com/kaiser-permanente-save-trees-gas-and-thrive/ (November 5, 2009).

7 Kaiser Permanente, News Center, Green Resource Center, http://xnet.kp.org/newscenter/aboutkp/green/index.html (April 12, 2010).

8 Ibid.

9 Southwest Airlines, Southwest.com, About, http://www.southwest.com/about_swa/?int=GFOOTER-ABOUT-ABOUT (Accessed October 2010).

10 Southwest Airlines, Culture, www.southwestairlines.com/careers/culture.html (April 20, 2010)

11 Joe Brancatelli, *Southwest Airlines' Seven Secrets for Success*, Portfolio.com at http://www.wired.com/cars/futuretransport/news/2008/07/portfolio_0708 (July 7, 2008)

12 Interbrand, GE Ecomagination, http://www.interbrand.com/case_study.aspx?caseid=1065&langid=1000, (April 5, 2010).

13 New Leaf Paper, Environmental Leadership and Sustainability, www.newleafpaper.com (November 5, 2009).

14 Investor Environmental Health Network, Case Studies, Rohner Textiles: Cradle-to-Cradle Innovation and Sustainability, http://www.iehn.org/publications.case.rohner.php (May 7, 2010).

15 Company Profile of Röhner Textile AG, http://www.climatex.com/de/story_d/hersteller/pdfs/Company_profile_engl.pdf (May 7, 2010)

16 William McDonough and Michael Braungart, Cradle to Cradle: Remaking the Way We Make Things, (New York, North Point Press), 2002, 107-108.

17 Investor Environmental Health Network, Case Studies, *Rohner Textiles: Cradle-to-Cradle Innovation and Sustainability*, http://www.iehn.org/publications.case.rohner.php (May 7, 2010).

18 William McDonough and Michael Braungart, *Cradle to Cradle: Remaking the Way We Make Things*, (New York, North Point Press), 2002, 108-109.

[19] Avon, Corporate Responsibility, http://responsibility.avoncompany.com/ (March 2, 2010).

[20] Hershey's, Discover Hershey®: Milton S. Hershey, http://www.hersheys.com/discover/milton/milton.asp (November 24, 2009).

[21] Ibid.

[22] The New York Job Source, Hershey Foods - Leading Maker of Chocolate and Candies, http://nyjobsource.com/hershey.html (January 24, 2008).

[23] All Business, *The Hershey Trust*, http://www.allbusiness.com/company-activities-management/board-management-changes/5503859-1.html, Originally Published *Food and Drink Weekly*, (November 19, 2007).

[24] Andrew Ross Sorkin, Hershey Trust Halts Auction Despite Offer of $12 Billion, *The New York Times*, http://www.nytimes.com/2002/09/18/business/18HERS.html (September 18, 2002).

[25] The Hershey Company, Making a Difference, http://www.thehersheycompany.com/social-responsibility/commitment.asp (February 20, 2010).

[26] John P. Kotter and James L. Heskett, *Corporate Culture and Performance*, (New York: Free Press, 1992), 11.

[27] Max Chafkin, "Get Happy," *Inc. Magazine*, May 2009, 69.

[28] Zappos.com, The Zappos Family Story - In the Beginning, http://about.zappos.com/zappos-story/in-the-beginning-let-there-be-shoes (November 11, 2009).

[29] Zappos.com, Our Unique Culture, http://about.zappos.com/our-unique-culture/zappos-core-values (November 11, 2009).

[30] Zappos.com, The Zappos Family Story - In the Beginning, http://about.zappos.com/zappos-story/in-the-beginning-let-there-be-shoes, (November 11, 2009)

[31] Gregory T. Huang, *$1.2B Amazon-Zappos Deal Closes*, Seattle PI Xconomy, http://www.xconomy.com/seattle/2009/11/02/1-2b-amazon-zappos-deal-closes/ (November 2, 2009).

[32] Candice Lombardi, *Zappos Tries Robots on for Size*, CNET News, Planetary Gear, http://news.cnet.com/8301-17912_3-9978844-72.html (June 27, 2008).

[33] Guy Kawasaki, *The Art of the Start*, (New York, Portfolio, 2004), 5.

[34] Lee J. Colan, *7 Moments that Define Excellent Leaders*, (Dallas, Cornerstone Leadership Institute, 2006), 17.

[35] Crane & Co., History, http://www.crane.com/navContentProduct.aspx?NavName=AboutUs&DeptName=History (May 10, 2010).

[36] Funding Universe, Company Histories: Crane & Co. Inc., http://www.fundinguniverse.com/company-histories/Crane-amp;-Co-Inc-Company-History.html (December 3, 2009).

[37] Adam Bluestein, "How We Did It - Crane & Co.," *Inc. Magazine*, October 2008, 122.

[38] Funding Universe, Company Histories: Crane & Co. Inc., http://www.fundinguniverse.com/company-histories/Crane-amp;-Co-Inc-Company-History.html (December 3, 2009).

[39] Ibid.

[40] Adam Bluestein, "How We Did It - Crane & Co.," *Inc. Magazine*, October 2008, 121.

41 Funding Universe, Company Histories: Crane & Co. Inc., http://www.fundinguniverse.com/company-histories/Crane-amp;-Co-Inc-Company-History.html (December 3, 2009).

42 Ibid.

43 Ibid.

44 Ibid.

45 Ibid.

46 Crane & Co., *Ever Green for 200 Years*, http://www.crane.com/greensince1801/ (May 25, 2010).

47 Spencer Johnson, MD, *Who Moved My Cheese?* (New York: Putnam, 2002).

48 Paul J.H. Schoemaker and Robert E. Gunther, "The Wisdom of Deliberate Mistakes," *Harvard Business Review*, June 2006.

49 Jill Bamberg, *Getting to Scale*, (San Francisco: Berrett-Koehler Publishers, Inc., 2006), 101.

50 Gary Hamel and C. K. Prahalad, *Competing for the Future*, (Boston: Harvard Business School Press, 1994), 79-116.

51 "Case Study: He Thought It Was Time to Shut Down Until His Workers Cooked Up a Scheme," *Inc. Magazine*, August 2008, 55-57.

52 Ibid.

53 Alex Salkever, "Has This Farmer Gone Bananas?" *Inc. Magazine*, August 2008, 54-57.

54 Daniel Goleman, Clarifications, "EI vs. IQ, Which is More Important?," http://danielgoleman.info/topics/emotional-intelligence/clarifications/ (Accessed October 2010).

55 *Associate Development: Enriching Our People*, Interface, http://www.interfaceglobal.com/Company/Culture/Strengths-Based-Culture.aspx (May 11, 2010).

56 Success Stories, Gallup, http://www.gallup.com/consulting/123695/Success-Stories.aspx (May 11, 2010).

57 Speakers Spotlight, Markus Buckingham, http://www.speakers.ca/buckingham_marcus.aspx (May 25, 2010).

58 Marcus Buckingham, *Now Discover Your Strengths*, (New York: Free Press, 2001), 48-61.

59 Certified B Corporation, B Corporation Directory, http://www.bcorporation.net/community/search (Accessed September 2011).

60 AISO.net, Company, Mission, http://www.aiso.net/company-mission.html (Accessed September 2010).

61 AISO.net, Technology, Sun Energized, http://www.aiso.net/technology-network-sun.html (Accessed September 2010).

62 AISO.net, Technology, Green Data Center, http://www.aiso.net/technology-green-data-center.html (Accessed September 2010).

63 Environmental Defense Fund, 2008 Innovations Review, http://www.edf.org/documents/7904_innovationsreview2008.pdf (Accessed September 2010).

64 Larry Kantor, "The Eco Advantage," *Inc. Magazine*, November 2006, http://www.inc.com/magazine/20061101/green50_intro.html (Accessed September 2010).

65 AISO.net, News, "AISO Becomes First Data Center to Join US Green Building Council," http://www.aiso.net/news-press-releases.html?id=8 (Accessed September 2010).

66 Environmental Defense Fund, 2008 Innovations Review, http://www.edf.org/documents/7904_innovationsreview2008.pdf (Accessed September 2010).

67 MSNBC.com, Environment, "Is Wal-Mart Going Green?," http://www.msnbc.msn.com/id/9815727/ (Accessed October 2010).

68 Wal-Mart Corporate, Global Sustainability Report, www.WalMartstores.com/sustainability/7951.aspx (Accessed October 2010).

69 See this great reference site on GRI- http://www.globalreporting.org/ReportingFramework/

70 Walmart, Global Sustainability Report 2010 Progress Update, Environment Overview, http://walmartstores.com/sites/sustainabilityreport/2010/environment_overview.aspx (Accessed October 2010).

71 Walmart, Global Sustainability Report 2010 Progress Update, Social, http://walmartstores.com/sites/sustainabilityreport/2010/social_internal_purchasing_practices.aspx (Accessed October 2010).

72 Interface, Sustainability, "The 7 Fronts of Mount Sustainability," http://www.interfaceglobal.com/Sustainability/Our-Journey/7-Fronts-of-Sustainability.aspx (Accessed October 2010).

73 The Walt Disney Company, Corporate Information, Company Overview, http://corporate.disney.go.com/corporate/overview.html (Accessed September 2010).

74 The Walt Disney Company, Disney Legends, Legends History, http://legends.disney.go.com/legends/about (Accessed September 2010).

75 The Walt Disney Company, Disney Legends, Directory, http://legends.disney.go.com/legends/direct?searchType=predef_specialty&Start=1&currPage=1 (Accessed January 2010).

76 Ign, PC, The Walt Disney Company Press Release, "Disney Gives Girls Slumber Party Tips to Celebrate the New Princess and the Frog Game," http://pc.ign.com/articles/105/1053989p1.html (Accessed September 2010).

77 The Walt Disney Company, 2008 Corporate Responsibility Report, http://disney.go.com/crreport/home.html (Accessed September 2010).

78 Jim Collins, *Good to Great: Why Some Companies Make the Leap and Others Don't*, (New York: HarperCollins Publishers Inc., 2001), 90-97.

79 Tom Kelly with Jonathan Littman, *The Art of Innovation*, (New York: Doubleday, 2001), 67-100.

80 Max Chafkin, "The Customer is the Company," Inc., http://www.inc.com/magazine/20080601/the-customer-is-the-company.html (Accessed June 2009).

81 Daniel Sitarz, *Greening Your Business*, (Carbondale, IL: EarthPress, 2008).

82 Michael Michalko, *Thinkertoys*, (Berkley, CA: Ten Speed Press, 2006).

83 John Taylor Gatto, "Against School: How Public Education Cripples Our Kids and Why," www.spinninglobe.net/againstschool.htm (Accessed September 2010).

84 Ray C. Anderson, Mid-Course Correction, Toward a Sustainable Enterprise: The Interface Model, (1998), 37-38.

85 Interface, Sustainability, "Our Mission," http://www.interfaceglobal.com/Sustainability/Our-Journey.aspx (Accessed September 2010).

86 Ray C. Anderson, Mid-Course Correction, *Toward a Sustainable Enterprise: The Interface Model*, (1998), 51-61.

87 Ibid, 71-75.

88 Interface, Sustainability, Global Ecometrics, http://www.interfaceglobal.com/getdoc/7e96b54e-ad49-4eff-9877-38a55df0396d/Global-EcoMetrics.aspx (Accessed September 2010).

89 The Natural Step, *ShoreBank Pacific: A Natural Step Network Case Study*, http://www.naturalstepusa.org/storage/case-studies/ShoreBank-toolkit.pdf (Accessed July 2010).

90 ShoreBank Pacific, *ShoreBank Pacific 2007-2008 Sustainability Report and Integrated Financials*, 2009. Further citations from this work are given in the text.

91 ShoreBank Pacific, *Putting Principles Into Action: Sustainability as Applied to Customers*, http://www.eco-bank.com/downloads/reports/criteria.pdf (Accessed July 2010).

92 One PacificCoast Bank, Sustainability, http://www.onepacificcoastbank.com/sustainability.aspx (Accessed August 2011).

93 ShoreBank Pacific, *ShoreBank Pacific 2006 Sustainability Report and Integrated Financials*, 2007.

94 James Sterngold, "ShoreBank of Chicago Said to Be Closed Today by FDIC," *Bloomberg*, August 20, 2010, http://www.bloomberg.com/news/2010-08-20/shorebank-of-chicago-said-to-be-closed-today-by-fdic.html (Accessed July 2011).

95 Christina Williams, "ShoreBank acquisition closed by OneCalifornia," *Sustainable Business Oregon*, Jan. 3, 2011, http://www.sustainablebusinessoregon.com/articles/2011/01/shorebank-acquisition-closed-by.html (Accessed July 2011).

96 Joel Makower, "Strategies for the Green Economy," (Keynote speaker, Kona-Kohala Chamber of Commerce 2009 Kuleana Green Business Conference, Kailua-Kona, HI, May 6, 2009).

97 Daniel G. Short and Glenn A. Welsh, *Fundamentals of Financial Accounting*, 6th ed. (Homewood, Il: Irwin, 1990), 9-10.

98 2007 figures calculated from: Taipei City Government, History, http://english.taipei.gov.tw/ct.asp?xItem=1084524&ctNode=29490&mp=100002 (Accessed August 2010).

99 Geography of Taiwan, Taiwan's Environmental Problems, http://twgeog.geo.ntnu.edu.tw/english/environment/environment_problems.htm, (Accessed August 2010).

100 Oscar Chung, "Taming a River," *Taiwan Review*, Conservation, http://taiwanreview.nat.gov.tw/ct.asp?xItem=729&CtNode=1364 (Accessed August 2010).

101 Yung-Jaan Lee and Ching-Ming Huang, *Sustainability Index for Taipei*, www.net-lanna.info/environment/Abstract/41015729.pdf (Accessed August 2010).

102 Robert N. Wise and Yuh-Chyurn Ding, "Taipei Eco City 2050 Vision," *Interplan* 88 (Summer 2009): 3-6.

103 Ibid.

104 Aba Bhattarai, Fast Company, "Fast Cities: Taipei, Taiwan," May 2009, http://www.fastcompany.com/magazine/135/fast-cities-taipei-taiwan.html (Accessed October 2010).

105 Jill Rosenblum, The Natural Step, "McDonald's Sweden - Case Study," http://www.rrfb.com/pages/Secondary%20pages/restaurant%20study/mcdonalds.html

106 Ibid.

[107] Monitor Talent, "Mats Lederhausen: Investor and Advisor to Purpose-Driven Enterprises," http://www.monitortalent.com/documents/lederhausen.pdf (Accessed October 2010).

[108] McDonald's Canada, Our Story, FAQ, http://www.mcdonalds.ca/en/aboutus/faq.aspx (Accessed October 2010).

[109] Daniel McGinn, Green Rankings: The 2009 List, *Newsweek*, http://greenrankings.newsweek.com/companies/view/mcdonald-s, Sept. 21, 2009.

[110] McDonald's, Careers, Hamburger University, http://www.aboutmcdonalds.com/mcd/careers/hamburger_university.html (Accessed October 2010).

[111] McDonald's, *McDonald's 2009 Corporate Responsibility Report*, http://www.aboutmcdonalds.com/mcd/csr/report.html (Accessed September 2010).

[112] Mc Donald's, *Global Best of Green 2010: Building a Better Business Through Effective Environmental Practices Around the World*, http://www.aboutmcdonalds.com/etc/medialib/aboutMcDonalds/socialresponsiblity.Par.11632.File.dat/2010_BOG.pdf (Accessed September 2010).

[113] United States EPA, "Food to Fuel: Pacific Biodiesel, Inc.," http://www.epa.gov/wastes/conserve/materials/organics/food/success/pac-bio.htm (Accessed October 2010).

[114] Pacific Biodiesel, www.pacificbiodiesel.com (Accessed October 2010). Further citations from this work are given in the text.

[115] Timberland, *Working Here*, http://www.timberland.com/corp/index.jsp?page=workingHere, (July 12, 2010).

[116] www.biodiesel.com

[117] See www.SustainableBusinessSystems.com for more information on the Systainership™ Log.

BIBLIOGRAPHY

The following entries may be useful to leaders interested in in-depth explorations of the principles of sustainability leadership and related topics on sustainability strategies, full engagement of employees, and thriving with triple-based profitability. The Endnotes contain additional excellent resources, including websites.

Abdullah, Sharif M. *Creating A World That Works for All.* San Francisco, CA 94111: Berrett-Koehler Publishers, Inc., 1999.

Anderson, Ray C. *Mid-Course Correction: Toward a Sustainable Enterprise: The Interface Model.* White River Junction, VT 05001: Chelsea Green Publishing Company, 2005.

Arena, Christine. *Cause for Success: 10 Companies That Put Profits Second and Came in First.* Novato, CA 94949: New World Library, 2004.

B Lab. *2009 B Corporation (TM) Annual Report.* A Supplement to Sustainable Industries: The business source for leaders of the New Economy, San Francisco, CA 94111: Sustainable Media Inc., 2009.

Bamburg, Jill. *Getting to Scale: Growing Your Business Without Selling Out.* San Francisco, CA 94101: Berrett-Koehler Publishers, Inc., 2006.

Bennis, Warren. *On Becoming a Leader.* Reading, MA: Perseus Books, 1989, Introduction to Paperback Edition 1994.

Blake, Dennis W. *Joy At Work: A Revolutionary Approach To Fun On The Job.* Seattle, WA 98127: PVG, 2005.

Buckingham, Marcus and Curt Coffman. *First Break All the Rules: What the World's Greatest Managers Do Differently.* New York, New York 10020: Simon & Schuster, 1999.

Buckingham, Marcus and Donald O.Clifton. *Now, Discover Your Strengths.* New York, New York 10020: The Free Press, 2001.

Canfield, Jack with Janet Switzer. *The Success Principles.* New York, New York 10022: HarperCollins Publishers Inc., 2005.

Collins, Jim. *Good to Great: Why Some Companies Make the Leap… and Others Don't.* New York, New York 10022: HarperCollins Publishers Inc., 2001.

Conley, Chip and Eric Friedenwald-Fishman. *Marketing That Matters: 10 Practices to Profit Your Business and Change the World.* San Francisco, CA 94104: Berrett-Koehler Publishers, Inc., 2006.

Covey, Stephen R. *The 8th Habit: From Effectiveness to Greatness.* New York, New York 10020: Free Press, 2004.

Deming, W. Edwards. *Out of Crisis.* Cambridge, MA 02139: Massachusetts Institute of Technology, Center for Advanced Engineering Study, 1982.

DePree, Max. *Leadership Is an Art*. New York, New York 10103: Dell Publishing, 1989.

Eisler, Riane. *The Power Of Partnership*. Novato, CA 94949: New World Library, 2002.

Epstein, Marc J. *Making Sustainability Work: Best Practices in Managing and Measuring Corporate Social, Environmental, and Economic Impacts*. San Fransicso, CA 94104: Berrett-Koehler Publishers, Inc., 2008.

Estes, Jonathan M. *Smart Green: How to Implement Sustainable Business Practices in Any Industry - And Make Money*. Hoboken, NJ 07030: John Wiley & Sons, Inc., 2009.

Esty, Daneil C. and Andrew S. Winston. *Green to Gold: How Smart Companies Use Environmental Strategy to Innovate, Create Value, and Build Competitive Advantage*. New Haven, CT: Yale University Press, 2006.

Farber, Steve. *The Radical Leap: A Personal Lesson in Extreme Leadership*. Chicago, IL 60606: Dearborn Trade Publishing, 2004.

Gelb, Michael J. *How To Think Like Leonardo DaVinci: Seven Steps To Genius Every Day*. New York, New York 10036: Dell Publishing, 1998.

Gerber, Michael. The E Myth Revisited: *Why Most Small Businesses Don't Work And What To Do About It*. New York, New York 10022: HarperCollins Publishers, Inc., 1995.

Gerzon, Mark. *Leading Through Conflict: How Successful Leaders Transform Differences into Opportunities*. Boston, MA 02163: Harvard Business School Press, 2006.

Gladwell, Malcolm. *The Tipping Point: How Little Things Can Make A Big Difference*. New York, New York 10020: Back Bay Books, 2000, 2002.

Hamel, Gary. *Competing for the Future*. Boston, MA: Harvard Business School Press, 1994.

Hart, Stuart L. "Beyond Greening: Strategies for a Sustainable World." In *Harvard Business Review on Green Business Strategy*, 99-124. Boston, MA 02163: Harvard Business School Publishing Corporation, 2007.

Harvard Business Review On Corporate Responsibility, A collection of articles previously published in the Harvard Business Review. Boston, MA 02163: Harvard Business School Publishing Corporation, 2003.

Hawken, Paul, Amory B. Lovins, L.Hunter Lovins. "A Road Map for Natural Capitalism." In *Harvard Business Review on Green Business Strategy*, 65-98. Boston, MA 02163: Harvard Business School Publishing Corporation, 2007.

Hitchcock, Darcy and Marsh Willard. *The Business Guide To Sustainabiltiy*. London, NW1 0JH, UK: Earthscan, 2006.

HRH The Prince of Wales Business & The Environment Programme. *The Reference Compemdium on Business Sustainability*. Cambridge, United Kingdom: The University of Cambridge Programme for Industry, 2003.

James, Sarah and Torbjörn Lahti. *The Natural Step for Communities: How Cities and Towns Can Change to Sustainable Practices*. Gabriola Island, British Columbia, Canada: New Society Publishers, 2004.

Jaworski, Joseph. Synchronicity: *The Inner Path of Leadership*. San Francisco, CA 94111: Berrett-Koehler Publishers, Inc., 1996, 1998.

Johnson, Spencer. *Who Moved My Cheese?: An A-Mazing Way To Deal With Change In Your Work And In Your Life.* New York, New York 10014: G. P. Putnam's Sons, 1998, 2002.

Kaplan, Robert S. and David P. Norton. *The Balanced Scorecard: Translating Strategy Into Action.* Boston, MA 02163: Harvard Business School Press, 1996.

Kawasaki, Guy. *The Art of the Start: The Time-Tested, Battle-Hardened Guide for Anyone Starting Anything.* New York, New York 10014: Portfolio, 2004.

Kelly, Tom with Jonathan Littman. *The Art Of Innovation.* New York, New York 10036: Doubleday, 2001.

Kim, W.Chan and Renèe Mauborgne. *Blue Ocean Strategy.* Boston, MA 02163: Harvard Business School Publishing Corporation, 2005.

Kotter, John. *Leading Change.* Boston, MA 02136: Harvard Business School Press, 1996.

Kouzes, James M. and Barry Z. Posner. *The Leadership Challenge.* San Francisco, CA 94103: Jossey-Bass, 2002.

Loehr, Jim and Tony Schwartz. *The Power of Full Engagement: Managing Energy, Not Time, Is The Key To High Performance and Personal Renewal.* New York, New York 10020: The Free Press, 2003.

Lundin, Stephen C., Harry Paul, and John Christensen. *Fish: A Remarkable Way to Boost Morale and Improve Results.* New York, New York 10023: Hyperion, 2000.

Makower, Joel with Cara Pike. *Strategies For The Green Economy: Opportunities and Challenges In The New World Of Busines.* New York, New York: McGraw-Hill, 2009.

McDonough, William and Michael Braungart. *Cradle To Cradle: Remaking The Way We Make Things.* New York, New York 10003: North Point Press, 2002.

Michalko, Michael. *Thinkertoys.* Berkeley, CA 94707: Ten Speed Press, 2006.

Nattrass, Brian and Mary Altomare. *The Natural Step For Business: Wealth, Ecology And The Revolutionary Corporation.* Gabriola Island, British Columbia, Canada: New Society Publishers, 1999.

Patterson, Kerry et al. *Influencer: The Power To Change Anything.* New York, New York 10020: McGraw-Hill, 2008.

Pink, Daniel H. *A Whole New Mind: Why Right Brainers Will Rule The Future.* New York, New York 10014: Penguin Group, 2005, 2006.

Richards, Dick. *Is Your Genius at Work?* Mountain View, CA 94043: Davies-Black Publishing, 2005.

Savitz, Andrew W. and Karl Weber. *The Triple Bottom Line: How Today's Best Run Companies Are Achieving Economic, Social, and Environmental Success - And How You Can Too.* San Francisco, CA: Jossey-Bass, A Wiley Imprint, 2006.

Sitarz, Daniel. *Greening Your Business: The Hands-on Guide To Creating a Successful and Sustainable Business.* Carbondale, IL 62901: Earthpress, 2008.

Tolle, Eckhart. *A New Earth: Awakening To Your Life's Purpose.* New York, New York, 10014: Plume, 2005.

Werbach, Adam. *Strategy For Sustainability: A Business Manifesto.* Boston, MA 02163: Harvard Business Press, 2009.

Willard, Bob. *The Next Sustainability Wave: Building Boardroom Buyin*. Gabriola Island, British Columbia, Canada: New Society Publishers, 2005.

Willard, Bob. *The Sustainability Advantage: Seven Business Case Benefits Of A Triple Bottom Line*. Gabriola Island, British Columbia, Canada: New Society Publishers, 2002.

Zander, Rosamund Stone and Benjamin Zander. *The Art of Possibility*. New York, New York 10014: Penguin Books, 2000.

INDEX

ABOUT THE AUTHOR

Lynn VanLeeuwen, ME, MS, ATPC, brings a visionary passion for sustainability with a career-long systems approach to business success. From her master's work at Harvard University in Business Management and Computer Systems to more than 20 years as a management design specialist and Wall Street consultant, Lynn's powerful skills are a perfect match for this vision.

As founder and principal of Sustainable Business Systems and creator of The Systainership™ Program, Lynn provides leadership tools and coaching for building sustainable organizations. A consummate designer of possibilities, she guides business executives and their companies to accelerate profitability through sustainable practices and systems.

For more information, visit www.SustainableBusinessSystems.com.

Promoting the Ripple Effect
of Conscious Business

QUICK ORDERING

To quickly order more copies of this book,
go to www.TheGreenCEO.com to link to your favorite seller.

Yes, I'm ready to improve the effectiveness of our sustainability initiatives!

Please send more information on:

- ❑ Systainership™
- ❑ Systainership™ Officers' Club
- ❑ Systainership™ Fast-Track Executive Coaching
- ❑ Scheduling a sustainability leadership strategy session
- ❑ Other: ____________________

My key challenges and frustrations are:

____

____

____

Name: ____________________

Company: ____________________

Address: ____________________

City: ____________________ State: ________ Zip: __________

Telephone: ____________________

Email address: ____________________

Number of employees: ____________________

Send postal requests to:
Sustainable Business Systems
PO Box 7209, Ocean View, HI 96737

Scan and email request to:
info@sustainablebusinesssystems.com

See www.SustainableBusinessSystems.com

www.ingramcontent.com/pod-product-compliance
Lightning Source LLC
LaVergne TN
LVHW091042080826
845145LV00002B/597

* 9 7 8 0 9 8 2 7 8 6 8 0 2 *